Annotated Teacher's Edition

WORLD OF VOCABULARY

RED

Sidney J. Rauch

Alfred B. Weinstein

Assisted by Muriel Harris

Photo Credits

p. 2: Photofest; **p. 5:** Photofest; **p. 7:** Photofest; **p. 8:** Smeal/Galella, Ltd.; **p. 11:** Smeal/Galella, Ltd.; **p. 13:** Sygma/Bill Nation; **p. 14:** Wide World Photos; **p. 17:** Wide World Photos; **p. 19:** Wide World Photos; **p. 20:** UPI/The Bettmann Archive; **p. 23:** UPI/The Bettmann Archive; **p. 25:** UPI/The Bettmann Archive; **p. 26:** Wide World Photos; **p. 29:** Wide World Photos; **p. 31:** Wide World Photos; **p. 32:** NASA; **p. 35:** UPI/The Bettmann Archive; **p. 37:** NASA; **p. 38:** Wide World Photos; **p. 41:** Wide World Photos; **p. 43:** Wide World Photos; **p. 44:** Wide World Photos; **p. 47:** Wide World Photos; **p. 49:** Wide World Photos; **p. 50:** Wide World Photos; **p. 53:** Wide World Photos; **p. 55:** Wide World Photos; **p. 56:** Ted Dargan/*St. Louis Post Dispatch*; **p. 59:** Ted Dargan/*St. Louis Post Dispatch*; **p. 61:** © Hazel Hankin/Stock Boston; **p. 62:** Wide World Photos; **p. 65:** Wide World Photos; **p. 67:** Wide World Photos; **p. 68:** ICM Artists Limited/Photo: Bill King; **p. 71:** ICM Artists Limited/Photo: Bill King; **p. 73:** © Walter Scott; **p. 74:** Smeal/Galella, Ltd.; **p. 77:** Smeal/Galella, Ltd.; **p. 79:** Photofest **p 80:** Reuters/Bettmann; **p. 83:** Reuters/Bettmann; **p. 85:** Soccer Industry Council of America; **p. 86:** Wide World Photos; **p. 89:** Wide World Photos; **p. 91:** Wide World Photos; **p. 92:** Wide World Photos; **p. 95:** Wide World Photos; **p. 97:** Wide World Photos; **p. 98:** UPI/The Bettmann Archive; **p. 101:** UPI/The Bettmann Archive; **p. 103:** © Bettye Lane; **p. 104:** Wide World Photos; **p. 107:** Wide World Photos; **p. 109:** Wide World Photos; **p. 116:** Sygma/Mark Weiss; **p. 119:** Sygma/Mark Weiss; **p. 121:** Photo Researchers/© Steve Kagan 1980.

World of Vocabulary, Red Level, Third Edition
Sidney J. Rauch • Alfred B. Weinstein

Printed in the United States of America

1 2 3 4 5 6 7 8 9 10   99 98 97 96

ISBN: 0-8359-1308-2

CONTENTS

>>>> Program Overview

The eight books in the *World of Vocabulary* series are especially designed to interest ESL/LEP students and students who have been reluctant or slow to expand their vocabularies. As an effective alternative to traditional vocabulary development programs, each lesson in *World of Vocabulary* offers:

- a short, high-interest, nonfiction article that incorporates the key words for that lesson in a meaningful context.
- photographs that hold students' attention and provide additional context for the key words.
- a variety of short skills exercises that build understanding and retention.
- high-interest writing and simple research projects that offer opportunities for students to extend their learning.

This revised edition of *World of Vocabulary* includes new and updated lessons at all levels. Changes in the design make the vocabulary lessons and instructions to students clearer and more approachable. New stories in all eight books spotlight personalities, such as Jim Carrey, Sandra Cisneros, and Steven Spielberg, and cover topics as engaging as World Cup soccer, Navajo code talkers, "Star Trek," and a group of Los Angeles teenagers who make and sell "Food from the 'Hood."

The revised series continues to offer diverse subjects and now includes selections on Latino actor Edward James Olmos, African American writer Walter Dean Myers, Native American ballerina Maria Tallchief, Latino baseball legend Roberto Clemente, Puerto Rican writer Nicholasa Mohr, and Chinese American writer Laurence Yep.

All eight books continue to have color designations rather than numbers to prevent students from identifying the books with grade levels. The use of color levels also enables teachers to provide individual students with the appropriate reading skills and vocabulary enhancement without calling attention to their reading levels. Below are the revised *World of Vocabulary* books listed by color and reading level:

Yellow	3
Tan	4
Aqua	5
Orange	6
Blue	7
Red	8
Purple	9
Green	10

As in the earlier version of *World of Vocabulary*, some lesson elements are carried throughout the series, but the pedagogy and design of each book is geared to the needs of students at that level. For example, the Yellow and Tan books are set in a larger typeface and have more write-on space for student responses than the other six books. Each lesson in these first two books contains eight key vocabulary words, compared to ten key words in the other books.

The Yellow and Tan books also include 15 units rather than the 20 units in the other books in the series. "Using Your Language" exercises in the Yellow and Tan books teach fundamental language skills that may need reinforcement at this reading level. The Tan book adds a phonics exercise.

As the reading level progresses in the next six books, the exercises offer more vocabulary words and increasing challenges. For example, "Find the Analogies" exercises appear in some lessons at the Aqua, Orange, and Red levels but are a part of every lesson in the Blue, Purple, and Green books.

>>>> The Need for Vocabulary Development

Learning depends on the comprehension and use of words. Students who learn new words and add them to their working vocabularies increase their chances for success in all subject areas.

Understanding new words is especially crucial for remedial and second-language learners. Their reluctance or inability to read makes it even more difficult for them to tackle unfamiliar words. The *World of Vocabulary* series was created for these students. The reading level of each selection is carefully controlled so students will not be burdened with an overload of new words.

Most importantly, the *World of Vocabulary* series motivates students by inviting them to relate their own experiences and ideas to the selections. In doing so, students gain essential practice in the interrelated skills of listening, speaking, reading, and writing. This practice and reinforcement enhances their vocabulary and language development.

>>>> Key Strategies Used in the Series

Providing Varied Experiences

The more varied experiences students have, the more meaning they can obtain from the printed word. For example, students who have studied the development of the space program will also have learned many new words, such as *astronaut* and *module*. They have also attached new meanings to old words, such as *shuttle* and *feedback*.

The reading selections in the *World of Vocabulary* series enable students to enrich their vocabulary by exploring major news events, as well as the lives and motivations of fascinating people. Through the wide range of selections, students encounter new words and learn different meanings of old words.

Visual tools are also valuable sources of experience. The full-page and smaller photographs in the lessons capture students' attention and help them to understand the words in the reading selections.

Building Motivation

If we can create the desire to read, we are on our way to successful teaching. Formal research and classroom experience have shown that the great majority of students are motivated to read if the following ingredients are present: opportunities for success, high-interest materials, appropriate reading levels, the chance to work at their own rate, and opportunities to share their experiences.

All of these ingredients are incorporated into the *World of Vocabulary* lessons through the use of engaging reading selections, controlled reading levels, a range of skills exercises, and discussion and enrichment opportunities.

Making Learning Meaningful

We do not often learn new words after one exposure, so vocabulary development requires repetition in meaningful situations. The *World of Vocabulary* series provides opportunities for students to use new words in relevant speaking and writing activities based on the high-interest reading selections.

Fostering Success

When students feel they have accomplished something, they want to continue. The *World of Vocabulary* series is designed to help students gain a feeling of accomplishment through listening, speaking, reading, and writing activities that motivate them to go beyond the lessons.

>>>> Readability Levels

The reading level in each lesson is controlled in two ways. First, vocabulary words appropriate to the designated reading level were selected from the EDL Core Vocabulary Cumulative List. The words were chosen for their interest, motivational level, and relevance to each reading selection.

Next, the reading level of each selection was adjusted using the Flesch-Kincaid Readability Index. This formula takes into account average sentence length, number of words per sentence, and number of syllables per word.

VOCABULARY STRATEGIES

>>>> Learning and Thinking Styles

People of all ages learn and think in different ways. For example, most of us receive information through our five senses, but each of us tends to prefer learning through one sense, such as our visual or auditory modality.

By keeping in mind the different ways students learn and think, we can appeal to the range of learning and thinking styles. By taking different styles into account in planning lessons, we can help all students understand new information and ideas and apply this knowledge and insight to their lives.

There are three main learning styles:

- Visual learners like to see ideas.
- Auditory learners prefer to hear information.
- Kinesthetic or tactile learners absorb concepts better when they can move about and use their hands to feel and manipulate objects.

After we receive information, we tend to process or think about the information in one of two ways:

- Global thinkers prefer to see the "big picture," the whole idea or the general pattern, before they think about the details. They search for relationships among ideas and like to make generalizations. They are especially interested in material that relates to their own lives. Global thinkers tend to be impulsive and quick to respond to teachers' questions.
- Analytical thinkers focus first on the parts and then put them together to form a whole. They think in a step-by-step approach and look at information in a more impersonal way. They are more likely to analyze information and ideas rather than apply it to their own lives. Analytical thinkers tend to be reflective and thoughtful in their answers.

However, few of us are *only* auditory learners or *only* analytical thinkers. Most people use a combination of learning and thinking styles but prefer one modality or style over the others. An effective lesson takes into account all three types of learning and both types of thinking. The ideas below, in addition to your own creativity, will help you meet the needs and preferences of every student in your class.

Visual Learners

- Write the lesson's key vocabulary words on the chalkboard, overhead transparency, or poster so students can see the words and refer to them.
- Encourage students to examine the photographs in the lesson and to explain what the pictures tell them about the key words.
- Repeat oral instructions or write them on the board. After giving instructions, put examples on the board.

- Involve students in creating word cluster maps (see p. xiv) to help them analyze word meanings.
- Use the other graphic organizers on pp. xiii-xvii to help students put analogies and other ideas into a visual form.
- Display some of the writing assignments students complete for the "Learn More About..." sections. Encourage students to read each other's work.
- For selections that focus on authors or artists, collect books, pictures, or other works by that author or artist for students to examine.
- For selections that focus on actors, show videotapes of their movies or television shows.

Auditory Learners

- Invite a volunteer to read aloud the selection at the beginning of each unit as students follow along in their books. You might audiotape the selection so students can listen to it again on their own.
- Ask a student to read aloud the "Understanding the Story" questions.
- Provide time for class and small-group discussions.
- Read aloud the directions printed in the books.
- Occasionally do an activity orally as a class, such as "Complete the Story."
- Allow students to make oral presentations or to audiotape assignments from the "Learn More About..." sections.

Kinesthetic or Tactile Learners

- Encourage students to take notes so the movements of their hands can help them learn new information.
- Encourage students to draw pictures to illustrate new words.
- In small groups, have students act out new words as they say the words aloud.
- Invite students to clap out the syllable patterns and/or spellings of new words.

- Write (or have students write) the new words on cards that can be handled and distributed.
- Provide sets of letters that students can arrange to spell the key words.

Global Thinkers

- Explain the "big picture," or the general idea, first.
- Point out how the key words fit patterns students have studied and how they relate to words and concepts that are already familiar to students.
- Involve students in brainstorming and discussion groups. Encourage students to express ideas and images that they associate with the new words.
- Explore ways that ideas and information are relevant to students.
- Encourage students to think about their answers before they respond.
- Set goals and offer reinforcement for meeting those goals.

Analytical Thinkers

- Start with the facts and then offer an overview of the topic.
- Give students time to think about their answers before they respond.
- Encourage students to set their own goals and to provide their own reinforcement for meeting them.
- Suggest that students classify new words into several different categories.
- Provide time for students to organize concepts or processes in a step-by-step approach.
- Help students recognize how new concepts relate to their own lives.

>>>> Cooperative Learning

One way to address multiple learning and thinking styles and to engage students more actively in their own learning is through cooperative learning activities.

Cooperative learning means more than having students work in groups. They must work together toward a shared goal that depends on each person's contribution. In cooperative learning, group members share ideas and materials, divide task responsibilities among themselves, rely on each other to complete these responsibilities, and are rewarded as a group for successful completion of a task.

If your students are not accustomed to group work, you might assign (or have students choose) group roles, such as discussion leader, recorder, reporter, or timekeeper. Having specific responsibilities will help group members work together.

Cooperative learning has many applications in the *World of Vocabulary* series. For instance, you might organize the class into groups and have each group teach its own members the key vocabulary words in that lesson. Groups could use a jigsaw approach, with each person learning and then teaching two or three words to other members of the group. Groups might create their own word searches, flashcards, crossword puzzles, incomplete sentences, analogies, and so on.

Then evaluate each group member to determine his or her level of understanding. Or you might ask group members to number off so you can evaluate only the 3s, for example. Explain that you will hold the entire group accountable for those students' mastery of the lesson words.

In other applications of cooperative learning, students might work together to create one product, such as a cluster map, a simple research project, or an original story that incorporates the key vocabulary words.

You might also consider trying the cooperative learning activities below, modifying them so they will be appropriate for your students.

Word Round-Robin

Organize the class into groups of ten (eight for Yellow and Tan levels) and have each group sit in a circle. Ask members to count off 1-10 (or 1-8) and give everyone a sheet of paper. Assign all the 1s one vocabulary word from the lesson, the 2s another word, and so on. Then follow these steps:

Step 1: Ask students to write their assigned word and their best guess as to its definition.

Step 2: Have students pass their papers to the person on their right. Then tell them to read through the story to find the word on the paper they received. Have students write another definition below the first definition on the paper, using context clues from the story.

Step 3: Ask students to pass their papers to their right. This time tell students to use a dictionary to look up the word on the paper they received. Then have them write on the paper the dictionary definition and a sentence that includes the word, using the same meaning as in the story.

Step 4: Invite groups to read each paper aloud, discuss the word, and write one definition in their own words, based on what members wrote on the papers.

Step 5: Have each group share its definition for the assigned word with the class. Discuss similarities and differences among the definitions. Guide students to recognize that definitions of some new words are clear even in isolation because of their root words, while others have multiple definitions that depend on the context in which they are used.

Synonym Seekers

Involve the class in preparing for this activity by assigning a vocabulary word to each pair of students. (You might include words from more than one selection.) Each pair will write its word and as many synonyms as possible on an index card, consulting a dictionary and thesaurus, if you wish.

Have pairs share their cards with the class, explaining subtle differences among the synonyms. Then collect the cards and combine pairs of students to form teams of four or six. Call out one of the vocabulary words and ask teams to write down as many synonyms as they can think of in 30 seconds.

Then read the synonyms listed on the card. Teams will give themselves one point for each synonym they recalled. Encourage students to suggest new synonyms to add to the cards and discuss why certain words could not be used as synonyms. Play the game several times with these cards before creating new cards with other words.

>>>> Approaches for ESL/LEP Students

- Invite volunteers to read the stories aloud while students follow along in their books.
- Watch for figurative expressions in the lessons and discuss their literal and intended meanings. Examples include "making faces," "friendly fire," and "bounce off the walls."
- Help students identify root words. Involve them in listing other words with the same roots and in exploring their meanings.
- Compare how prefixes and suffixes in the vocabulary words are similar to those in words students already know.
- Make word webs to help students understand relationships among words and concepts. Use the graphic organizer on page xiv or write a vocabulary word in the center of the chalkboard or poster. Invite students to name as many related words as possible for you to write around the key word. Discuss how each word is related.
- Involve students in listing words that are similar in some way to a vocabulary word, such as other vehicles, adverbs, occupations, and so on.
- Encourage students to share words or phrases from their native languages that mean the same as the vocabulary words. Invite them to teach these words from their native languages to the class.
- Arrange cooperative learning and other activities so ESL/LEP students are grouped with students who speak fluent English.
- Periodically group ESL/LEP students together so that they can assist one another in their native languages.
- Foster discussion with questions, such as "Do you think our space program should send more astronauts to the moon? Why?" and "Would you like to perform in a circus? Why?" These kinds of questions encourage students to use English to share their ideas and opinions.

>>>> Cross-Curricular Connections

General
- Challenge students to identify vocabulary words that have different meanings in other subject areas. For example, *fins* are defined as "rubber flippers" in the Aqua book. How are *fins* defined in science?
- Give extra credit to students who find the lesson's vocabulary words in other textbooks or in newspapers and magazines. Discuss whether the meaning is the same in both uses.

Math
- Invite pairs of students to write problems that include vocabulary words. The difficulty level will depend on their math skills. Ask pairs to exchange problems and try to solve each others'.

Language Arts
- Encourage students to write letters to some of the people described in the stories. Ask them to incorporate some of the lesson's key words into their letters.
- Have students, working in pairs or individually, write their own stories, using a certain number of vocabulary words from one or more selections.

They might leave the spaces blank and challenge other students to complete the stories correctly.

- Organize a spelling contest, using vocabulary words.
- Have groups prepare crossword puzzles that will be combined into a book.
- Encourage students to conduct surveys and/or interview people regarding topics that stem from the stories. For example, how many students or staff at school collect trading cards? What kinds do they collect? How many students or staff are "Star Trek" fans? What attracts them to "Star Trek"? Encourage students to graph their findings and to write short reports explaining their conclusions.

A SAMPLE LESSON PLAN

The following is a suggested plan for teaching a lesson from the *World of Vocabulary* series. You might use it as a guide for preparing and organizing your lessons. However, be sure to modify it where necessary to take into account your students' needs, abilities, interests, and learning styles, along with the specific exercises included in that lesson.

>>>> Setting Objectives

Each lesson in the *World of Vocabulary* series is based on the objectives below.
- To create enthusiasm for and an understanding of the importance of learning new words
- To improve reading comprehension by teaching the meanings of new words, stressing context clues
- To improve vocabulary by presenting key words in exercises that range from simple to complex and that allow for reinforcement of learning
- To encourage oral expression and motivate further study by introducing a highly interesting topic.

>>>> Stimulating Interest

Invite students to examine the photograph on the first page of the lesson. To stimulate their curiosity and involve them in the topic, ask questions. For example, if the lesson were about Koko the gorilla, you might ask:
- The gorilla in the picture is named Koko. How do you think Koko might be different from other gorillas?
- Do you think it is possible to teach a gorilla to talk? Why or why not?
- If Koko could talk to people, what do you think she might say?

>>>> Reading the Story

Have students read the story, silently or in small groups. You also might assign the story to be read outside class. To help auditory learners and ESL/LEP students, ask a volunteer to read the story aloud while classmates follow along in their books.

Encourage students to use the context clues in the story and the opening photograph to figure out the meanings of several boldfaced words. You might have students suggest a definition for each key word, based on context clues. Write the definitions on the chalkboard so the class can review and modify them later in the lesson.

As an aid to ESL/LEP students, discuss words or phrases in the story that have more than one meaning or that have figurative meanings. Two examples in the story about Koko are "blew kisses" and "spends some time."

>>>> Completing the Exercises

The information about exercises below is based on the lesson about Koko in the Orange level. However, books at different levels include different exercises. For example, the Yellow and Tan books offer a simpler activity called "Make a List" instead of the "Understanding the Story" exercise.

Students using the Yellow and Tan books also complete an exercise called "Find the Synonyms," while students at the Aqua, Orange, and Red levels have the "Complete the Sentences" exercise. The equivalent exercise for students at the Blue, Purple, and Green levels is called "Find the Analogies." Each level also includes a variety of other grammar and skills exercises.

Despite variations in exercises from level to level, the explanations below will help you understand why certain exercises are included and how they can be modified to support different learning and thinking styles.

>>>> "Understanding the Story"

This exercise usually asks students to determine the main idea of the selection and to make an inference as a way of assessing their general understanding of the story. Remember that global thinkers may have an easier time describing the main idea than analytical thinkers, who tend to focus on the parts of the story rather than the whole idea.

To use this as a cooperative activity, have students discuss the questions in groups of two or three. Then pair two groups so they can share their conclusions. Ask groups that disagreed on the answers to tell the class the reasoning for their different choices. Be sure to clear up any misunderstandings that become apparent without squelching creativity.

To make sure all students understand the general content of the story, ask a volunteer to summarize it in a sentence or two. Then give the analytical thinkers in the class an opportunity to contribute by describing some of the key supporting details in the story.

>>>> "Make an Alphabetical List"

This activity encourages students to study the key words closely and to become more familiar with their spellings. Practicing writing the words in alphabetical order will be especially beneficial for kinesthetic learners.

To check students' accuracy in arranging the words in alphabetical order, ask one or two students to read their lists aloud. Visual learners will appreciate seeing the list written on the board.

If necessary, model the pronunciation of certain words. Practice saying the more difficult words as a class. (This technique will also be helpful for ESL/LEP students.)

>>>> "What Do the Words Mean?"

In this exercise, students match the definitions listed in their books to the lesson's vocabulary words. If students offer other definitions for the same words, encourage them to consult a dictionary to check their accuracy. Many of the key words have different meanings in other contexts.

Encourage students to suggest synonyms for the words and perhaps some antonyms. Analytical learners might enjoy identifying root words and listing other words with the same roots, prefixes, or suffixes. Many ESL/LEP students will also benefit from this analysis.

>>>> "Complete the Sentences"

This exercise gives students another opportunity to practice using context clues as they complete a set of sentences using the key words.

>>>> "Use Your Own Words"

Working individually or in groups, students are encouraged to brainstorm words that describe a picture or express their reactions to it. This exercise fosters creativity involves students in the lesson by asking for their personal responses. Their responses will depend on their prior knowledge and individual perceptions, so answers are not included in the Answer Key. You might use some of the graphic organizers on pages xiii–xvii for this activity.

As a cooperative activity, students might enjoy working with three classmates to write a group description of the picture. Tell the first group member to write a word related to the picture on a sheet of paper and to pass the paper to the right. Have the next two group members add their own words, different from the ones already listed. Then ask the fourth group member to write one sentence about the picture that includes all three words. Start another sheet of paper with a different group member and continue in the same way, with the fourth member combining the words into one sentence.

>>>> "Make New Words from Old"

This is one of several reinforcement exercises throughout the *World of Vocabulary* series. "Make New Words from Old" invites students to look creatively at the letters in a key word from the lesson. Other exercises in the series challenge students to identify synonyms and/or antonyms, underline specific parts of speech, to find the subjects and predicates in sentences, to write the possessive forms of words, or to complete other activities that focus on key words from the lesson.

>>>> "Complete the Story"

Students again use context clues to place the lesson's key words correctly in a new story. This story relates to the one that opened the lesson and may offer more information on the topic or encourage students to apply new knowledge or insights in their own lives. You might use "Complete the Story" as a post-test of student mastery of the key words.

>>>> "Learn More About..."

The last page of each lesson offers one to four activities that encourage students to learn more about the lesson's topic. You might assign one or several activities or encourage students to choose an activity to complete for extra credit. They could work during class time or outside of class—individually, with partners, or in small groups.

Some of the activities are developed for ESL/LEP students, while others provide opportunities for cooperative learning, cross-curricular projects, and enrichment. Placing activities in these categories was not meant to limit their use, as many of the activities would benefit and interest most students. For some reluctant readers, these projects may be their first attempt at independent research, fueled by their interest in the lesson's topic.

Some lessons include a "Further Reading" activity that lists fiction or nonfiction books on the lesson's topic that are appropriate for that reading level. Students are asked to complete a brief activity after their reading.

"Further Reading" and other activities that require a written response provide additional opportunities for students to practice and receive feedback on their writing skills, including punctuation, capitalization, and spelling. The effort students spend on the "Learn More About" activities can result in marked improvements in their reading and writing skills.

UNDERSTANDING THE STORY

>>>> The topic of the story:

>>>> The main idea of the story:

>>>> Some details from the story:

>>>> What interested me most:

>>>> A question I would like to ask:

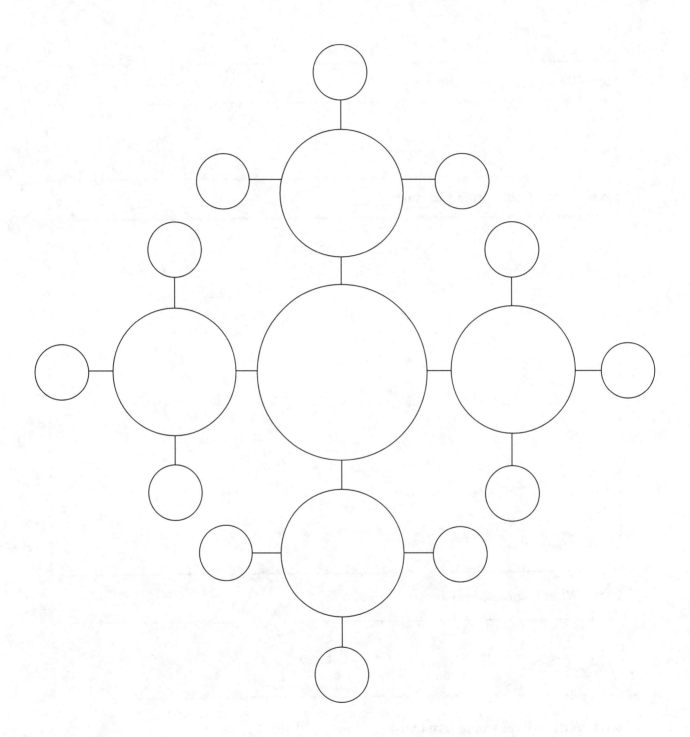

A _____ is a _____ that
    (key word)   (description)

_____, _____, and
(characteristic)   (characteristic)

_____.
(characteristic)

relationship

_____ is to _____ ☐ as _____ is to _____.

relationship

_____ is to _____ ☐ as _____ is to _____.

relationship

_____ is to _____ ☐ as _____ is to _____.

relationship

_____ is to _____ ☐ as _____ is to _____.

relationship

_____ is to _____ ☐ as _____ is to _____.

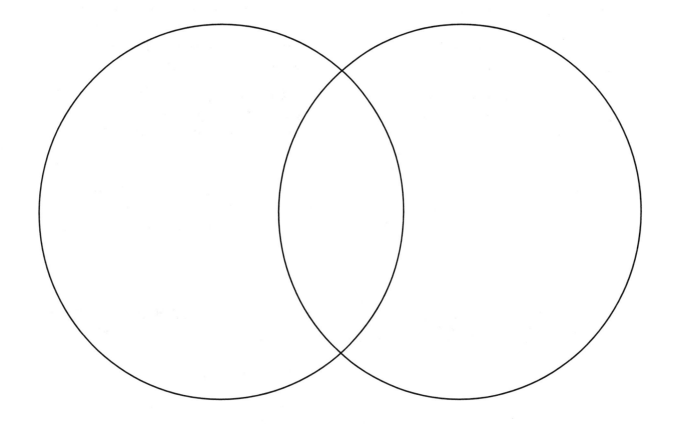

Understanding the Story (page xiii)

This form will help students analyze the selection at the beginning of each unit and organize its content logically and visually.

Cluster Map (page xiv)

This organizer will help structure individual or group brainstorming sessions. Students write a key word or concept in the middle circle and related words or concepts in the adjoining circles.

Word Chart (page xv)

Students can use this chart to compare key words with similar words. They write words in the first column on the left and list categories across the top of the chart.

In another use of the chart, students might write adjectives in the left column. Across the top, they could list experiences.

Analogy Organizer (page xvi)

Students write in the box the relationship between the words in each pair. Then they write the three words given in the analogy in the blank spaces and choose a word listed in the book to complete the analogy. You might also use this graphic organizer to help students write their own analogies.

Venn Diagram (page xvii)

This organizer offers another way to compare the meanings of similar words. Students write the words to be compared above each circle. Then they list several properties that apply only to each word inside the circle and properties that the words share in the center area.

Red Test Answers

1. morbid
2. embellishes
3. prosperity
4. creed
5. sponsored
6. tenants
7. undeniable
8. contemporary
9. recovery
10. maverick
11. corridor
12. neglected
13. combination
14. literature
15. fantasy
16. incentive
17. glamour
18. sequence
19. propels
20. revived
21. intriguing
22. amiable
23. tarnished
24. adjusted
25. insight
26. astonished
27. conscientious
28. magnitude
29. possibility
30. subtle
31. technique
32. verify
33. excel

RED TEST

WHAT DO THE WORDS MEAN?

 Following are some meanings, or definitions, for the ten vocabulary words in the box below. Write the words next to their definitions.

prosperity	tenants	embellishes	sponsored	recovery
morbid	maverick	creed	undeniable	contemporary

1. _____ very gloomy
2. _____ makes more beautiful by adding something
3. _____ wealth; success
4. _____ a statement or belief
5. _____ supported; helped
6. _____ renters; people who occupy property owned by another
7. _____ plainly true; not questionable
8. _____ modern; of today
9. _____ a return to normal
10. _____ a person who doesn't go along with the crowd

COMPLETE THE SENTENCES

>>>> *Use the vocabulary words in this lesson to complete the following sentences. Use each word only once.*

combination	fantasy	revived	propels	incentive
sequence	corridor	glamour	literature	neglected

11. Chris was waiting for me in the _____.

12. I put the cake in the oven, but I _____ to set the timer.

13. The recipe called for an odd _____ of ingredients.

14. I enjoy reading a variety of _____.

15. I prefer reading science fiction and _____ over nonfiction.

16. Making the track team is my _____ for running every morning.

17. There is not a lot of _____ in running through the morning fog.

18. I warm up by doing stretching exercises in a certain _____.

19. The push of your toes against the track _____ your body forward.

20. After a hard run, I feel alive and _____.

FIND THE ANALOGIES

>>>> An **analogy** is a relationship between pairs of words. Here's one kind of analogy: *raindrop* is to *wet* as *sunlight* is to *hot*. In this relationship, the first word in each pair is an object, and the second word in each pair describes the object. See if you can complete the following analogies. Circle the correct word or words.

21. **Advocate** is to **dedicated** as **idea** is to

    a. person   b. intriguing   c. plan   d. creed

22. **Nation** is to **impoverished** as **friend** is to

    a. country   b. amiable   c. companion   d. culture

23. **Wood** is to **ignited** as **silver** is to

    a. gold   b. forested   c. timber   d. tarnished

COMPLETE THE STORY

>>>> *Use words from the box to fill in the blanks and complete the story. Use each word only once.*

magnitude	insight	verify	astonished	technique
adjusted	subtle	excel	possibility	conscientious

    My younger sister will be starting high school next year. I have already **(24)** _____ to the challenges of high school, so I will try to share an **(25)** _____ or two with her. For example, during my first week at Westview High, I was **(26)** _____ at the reading assignments. I tried to be **(27)** _____ and read every word, but the **(28)** _____ of the task overwhelmed me.

    As the **(29)** _____ of my failing history entered the picture, I learned **(30)** _____ little strategies that helped me read faster. One **(31)** _____ was to look for topic sentences and key words as I read. Another was to predict what a section would cover and then **(32)** _____ my predictions after I had read the section. Although I still did not exactly **(33)** _____ in history, I did pass!

CONTENTS

1 NATIVE AMERICAN ACTOR

A veteran of Vietnam and a full-blooded Cherokee, Wes Studi—better known to the public as Geronimo—uses acting to express his anger about the way people treat each other. While a soldier in Vietnam, Studi saw *ample* proof of the horrors of war. His company nearly became *casualties* of "friendly fire" from fellow American soldiers.

After his *discharge* from the army, Studi spent several aimless years recovering from the experience. Then he focused his anger, both about the Vietnam War and the prejudice toward his people. He became an *advocate* for Native Americans and joined protests in Washington, D.C., and other cities. Although Studi spent several days in jail as a result of his actions, he feels no *remorse.* He thinks his protests were a way to complete his *recovery* from his experiences in Vietnam.

Studi worked as a newspaper reporter for a while but then turned to acting. He had roles in *The Last of the Mohicans* and *Dances with Wolves.* He had the starring role in *Geronimo: An American Legend.* Often ferocious on screen, Studi is actually a devoted father and a charming, *amiable* person.

In his movies, Studi insists that Native Americans be portrayed as real adults, not *alcoholic* children. He attacks his own roles with *zeal,* pouring his feelings into them. Studi would now like to play a different type of role. One *possibility* would be to play a Native American in the 21st century. He believes that his people will be around then, just like everyone else.

UNDERSTANDING THE STORY

>>>> *Circle the letter next to each correct statement.*

1. The statement that best expresses the main idea of this selection is:
   a. Native American movie roles are best played by people who have a Native American background.
   b. In his movie roles, Wes Studi uses emotions based on his own experiences.
   c. Wes Studi was deeply disturbed by his experiences in Vietnam.

2. From this story, you can conclude that
   a. Studi would like to play a character who is not a Native American.
   b. Studi believes that prejudice against Native Americans is a thing of the past.
   c. Wes Studi has been an inspiration to other Native Americans.

MAKE AN ALPHABETICAL LIST

>>>> *Here are the ten vocabulary words in this lesson. Write them in alphabetical order in the spaces below.*

possibility	zeal	advocate	recovery	ample
alcoholic	remorse	discharge	casualties	amiable

1. advocate
2. alcoholic
3. amiable
4. ample
5. casualties

6. discharge
7. possibility
8. recovery
9. remorse
10. zeal

WHAT DO THE WORDS MEAN?

>>>> *Following are some meanings, or definitions, for the ten vocabulary words in this lesson. Write the words next to their definitions.*

1. ample — full or enough; generous; plenty of something

2. remorse — a disturbing feeling of guilt

3. discharge — to let go

4. advocate — a person who defends or stands up for other people or a cause

5. amiable — agreeable; friendly

6. zeal — eagerness; passion

7. recovery — a return to normal

8. casualties — people who have been harmed or killed

9. alcoholic — a person who is dependent on alcohol

10. possibility — something that may happen

4

COMPLETE THE SENTENCES

>>>> *Use the vocabulary words in this lesson to complete the following sentences. Use each word only once.*

| possibility | zeal | advocate | recovery | ample |
| alcoholic | remorse | discharge | casualties | amiable |

1. During the Vietnam War, there were many deaths and other ____casualties____.

2. War offers ____ample____ evidence of the brutal ways people treat each other.

3. Wes Studi's ____recovery____ from his experiences in Vietnam took several years.

4. Studi's gentle personality off screen often conceals his energy and ____zeal____ for helping his people.

5. Despite his violent movie roles, Studi is friendly and ____amiable____.

6. Wes Studi did not know what to do with his life after his ____discharge____ from the army.

7. Studi became involved in protests that broke the law, but he feels no ____remorse____.

8. Eventually, Studi decided to become an ____advocate____ for Native Americans.

9. In his movies, Studi makes sure that Native Americans are not shown as a lazy, ____alcoholic____ group.

10. Studi is always interested in the ____possibility____ of new movie roles.

USE YOUR OWN WORDS

>>>> *Look at the picture. What words come into your mind? Write them on the lines below. To help you get started, here are two good words:*

1. ____warrior____
2. ____proud____
3. ____Answers will vary.____
4. _____
5. _____
6. _____
7. _____
8. _____
9. _____
10. _____

5

FIND THE ADJECTIVES

>>>> An **adjective** is a word that describes a person, place, or thing. The adjectives in the following sentences are underlined: The <u>excited</u> audience cheered (person). Studi was born in a <u>small</u> city in Oklahoma (place). I love <u>action</u> movies (thing).

>>>> *Underline the adjectives in the following sentences.*

1. Wes Studi is a <u>dedicated</u> and <u>enthusiastic</u> actor.
2. A <u>meaningful</u> movie can help change <u>public</u> opinion.
3. <u>Eager</u> fans await the <u>next</u> movie starring Studi.
4. Serving in Vietnam had a <u>profound</u> influence on the <u>young</u> Wes Studi.
5. Studi is a <u>proud</u> member of the <u>Cherokee</u> nation.

COMPLETE THE STORY

>>>> Here are the ten vocabulary words for this lesson:

remorse	advocate	casualties	zeal	possibility
discharge	recovery	amiable	alcoholic	ample

>>>> *There are six blank spaces in the story below. Four vocabulary words have already been used in the story. They are underlined. Use the other six words to fill in the blanks.*

The Vietnam War had even more ___casualties___ than the soldiers who were injured or killed there. Many soldiers returned to their former lives after <u>discharge</u> from the service. Yet, an ___ample___ number felt a good deal of ___remorse___ because of things that happened in Vietnam. Their <u>recovery</u> has taken years.

Wes Studi decided to use his anger by becoming an ___advocate___ for his people. He did not want anyone shown as an <u>alcoholic</u> in the movies. He wanted everyone to realize that each Native American is an individual, a real person. Studi's <u>zeal</u> has increased the ___possibility___ that other Native Americans will pursue their dreams. Behind that stern face is an ___amiable___ man who cares deeply about others.

Learn More About Native Americans

>>>> *On a separate sheet of paper or in your notebook or journal, complete one or more of the activities below.*

Appreciating Diversity

Many Native American groups used art as a form of communication. Try to find examples of different forms of Native American art, such as pictographs or designs used in pottery and clothing. Choose a few favorites and explain what the drawings mean to you.

Learning Across the Curriculum

Find out about the groups of Native Americans that live or used to live in your region. Research how their ancestors lived and what they valued. Write a comparison of how their ways are similar to and different from the ways of people in your region today.

Broadening Your Understanding

Learn more about other Native American actors, artists, and athletes, such as Jim Thorpe, Floyd Red Crow Westerman, Kevin Red Star, Graham Greene, Rodney Grant, and Cher. Share what you learn with the class.

2 THE TALENTED MS. STREEP

"Haunting, *lyrical,* *gripping,* and heartbreaking." These were some of the *comments* critics made about Meryl Streep's acting in *Sophie's Choice.* They praised the film, but it was Streep's acting that overwhelmed them. One reviewer *uttered* the feelings of many. He said, "The film has a performance by Meryl Streep that makes her an immortal." Thus Streep has captured the world with her *subtle* artistry. She is recognized as one of our greatest actresses.

Streep started acting as a high school student in New Jersey. From there, she went on to Vassar College and then to Yale Drama School. She played dozens of roles and kept polishing her skills.

The three films that display the best of Streep's art are *Out of Africa, A Cry in the Dark,* and *Sophie's Choice.* In each she *assumes* a different type of role. In *Out of Africa,* she's a strong-willed woman running a farm in Africa. In *A Cry in the Dark,* she's a woman *wrongfully* accused of murder. In *Sophie's Choice,* she's a Polish woman who manages to survive the horrors of a concentration camp. In all three films, Streep *elevates* the art of acting to its highest level. So far, she has received two Academy Awards for her work.

Offstage, Streep displays little show-business *glamour.* She enjoys spending time at home in New York with her family. However, she's still an actress concerned with *perfecting* her craft. The thought of what she is capable of doing in the future staggers the imagination.

UNDERSTANDING THE STORY

>>>> *Circle the letter next to each correct statement.*

1. The statement that best expresses the main idea of this selection is:
   a. The film *Sophie's Choice* received great reviews.
   b. Meryl Streep is an unusually gifted actress.
   c. Meryl Streep enjoys playing a different type of role in each film she makes.

2. The final sentence, "The thought of what she is capable of doing in the future staggers the imagination," really means that
   a. it takes a good imagination to predict Streep's future.
   b. Streep must continue to work at perfecting her art.
   c. Meryl Streep will reach even higher levels of excellence with each performance.

MAKE AN ALPHABETICAL LIST

>>>> *Here are the ten vocabulary words in this lesson. Write them in alphabetical order in the spaces below.*

subtle	lyrical	assumes	uttered	gripping
glamour	perfecting	elevates	wrongfully	comments

1. assumes
2. comments
3. elevates
4. glamour
5. gripping

6. lyrical
7. perfecting
8. subtle
9. uttered
10. wrongfully

WHAT DO THE WORDS MEAN?

>>>> *Following are some meanings, or definitions, for the ten vocabulary words in this lesson. Write the words next to their definitions.*

1. elevates — raises to a higher level; improves

2. wrongfully — unjustly; unfairly

3. assumes — takes over; undertakes

4. glamour — exciting attractiveness; fascinating personal style

5. gripping — strongly holding one's attention; fascinating

6. lyrical — song-like; poetic

7. comments — explanatory remarks; critical observations

8. perfecting — improving; bringing nearer to perfection

9. uttered — pronounced; spoken

10. subtle — skillful; artful; delicately crafted

10

COMPLETE THE SENTENCES

>>>> *Use the vocabulary words in this lesson to complete the following sentences. Use each word only once.*

glamour	gripping	elevates	lyrical	perfecting
comments	assumes	subtle	wrongfully	uttered

1. Even though the critics praise her, Streep goes on steadily _____perfecting_____ her art.

2. The _____glamour_____ of show business has little appeal for Meryl Streep.

3. To appreciate her acting, watch the _____subtle_____ movements of her eyes and hands.

4. *A Cry in the Dark* is a _____gripping_____ drama about a terrible crime.

5. Streep plays a woman _____wrongfully_____ accused of murder.

6. Critics use the term _____lyrical_____ to describe Meryl Streep because her acting is so full of poetic feeling.

7. A good actor or actress _____assumes_____ all the characteristics of the person being portrayed.

8. A word often _____uttered_____ to describe Meryl Streep is *magnificent*.

9. After a movie, it's always interesting to listen to people's _____comments_____.

10. Meryl Streep _____elevates_____ acting to a fine art.

USE YOUR OWN WORDS

>>>> *Look at the picture. What words come into your mind? Write them on the lines below. To help you get started, here are two good words:*

1. _____smile_____
2. _____earrings_____
3. ____Answers will vary.____
4. _____
5. _____
6. _____
7. _____
8. _____
9. _____
10. _____

11

FIND THE SUBJECTS AND PREDICATES

>>>> The **subject** of a sentence names the person, place, or thing that is spoken about. The **predicate** of a sentence is what is said about the subject. For example:

> The small boy went to the football game.

The small boy is the subject (the person the sentence is talking about). *Went to the football game* is the predicate of the sentence (because it tells what the small boy did).

>>>> *In the following sentences, draw one line under the subject of the sentence and two lines under the predicate of the sentence.*

1. Meryl Streep played a Polish woman in *Sophie's Choice.*
2. She is recognized by many critics as one of our greatest actresses.
3. Streep's acting simply took the critics by storm.
4. Streep lives in New York City, far from the exciting life of Hollywood.
5. Yale Drama School gave Streep many chances to perform in student plays.

COMPLETE THE STORY

>>>> Here are the ten vocabulary words for this lesson:

wrongfully	gripping	subtle	assumes	glamour
perfecting	elevates	lyrical	uttered	comments

>>>> *There are six blank spaces in the story below. Four vocabulary words have already been used in the story. They are underlined. Use the other six words to fill in the blanks.*

In addition to her many films, Meryl Streep appeared in the gripping TV movie *Holocaust*. The reviews of her performance were almost _____lyrical_____ in their praise. Streep's _____subtle_____ expressions showed her characters' inner feelings. One critic said, "The way she assumes both the inner and outer qualities of the person she is playing _____elevates_____ acting to a high art."

Away from the movie set, Streep quickly sheds the glamour of show business. She prepares for new roles by quietly _____perfecting_____ her skills. She has been _____wrongfully_____ accused by some critics of taking on too many different types of roles. One reviewer _____uttered_____ the comments of millions when he said, "There is greatness in the extraordinary acting of Meryl Streep."

Learn More About the Academy Awards

>>>> *On a separate sheet of paper or in your notebook or journal, complete one or more of the activities below.*

Building Language

Research movies in your native language that have won an Academy Award for Best Foreign Language Film. Find out more about one of the movies and present a report on it to your class. If you can, watch the movie and include a plot summary in your report.

Working Together

Divide into teams to create questions for an Academy Awards trivia contest. Each group will research questions about a particular category, such as winners of the best-picture awards, best-actor and best-actress awards, and the awards' history. After you have finished creating the questions, see how well your team does at answering the questions from the other teams.

Learning Across the Curriculum

Imagine you are in charge of updating the award the academy hands out. The officials of the academy have said they want something new—not a statue of a person. They say they want an award that reflects the spirit of the movies. Design a new award.

14

3 A SPECIAL WORLD

Welcome to a land of fun and *fantasy.* Welcome to the very special world of the Magic Kingdom, Epcot Center, and Disney MGM Studios. Welcome to Walt Disney World!

You will see Cinderella's Castle, *animated* sea creatures, and bright fireworks. You can stroll along Main Street, U.S.A., a *replica* of a small American town in the 1890s, thrill to the *illusion* of ghosts in the Haunted Mansion, and ride an elephant through a *menacing* jungle. It is all here in Disney World.

This *formidable* playland is twice the size of Manhattan—43 square miles. It has five lakes, three golf courses, two railroads, and a *monorail.* There are 50 miles of *navigable* waterways with 256 boats. Disney World even has its own telephone company, laundry, and fire department.

Epcot Center (*E*nvironmental *P*rototype *C*ommunity *o*f *T*omorrow) is Disney's vision of the future. There you can *maneuver* *Spaceship Earth* on a journey through time.

At Disney-MGM Studios, you can visit Hollywood Boulevard and take the Great Movie Ride, a sightseeing tour of cinematic wonders. Then create your own sound effects for a haunted-house film in the Monster Sound Show.

All these wonders and more are brought to you courtesy of Walt Disney, the *ingenious* king of adventure and imagination.

UNDERSTANDING THE STORY

>>>> *Circle the letter next to each correct statement.*

1. The statement that best expresses the main idea of this selection is:
   a. Walt Disney World is a fantastic kingdom, full of adventure and fun for all.
   b. Walt Disney's creation, Walt Disney World, is a tribute to Main Street U.S.A.
   c. Florida has become a popular resort mainly because of Disney World.

2. From this story, you can conclude that
   a. Walt Disney World is worth visiting because it is unique.
   b. only children and teenagers would enjoy visiting Walt Disney World.
   c. places like Walt Disney World are being built all over the world.

15

MAKE AN ALPHABETICAL LIST

>>>> *Here are the ten vocabulary words in this lesson. Write them in alphabetical order in the spaces below.*

menacing	ingenious	formidable	animated	fantasy
maneuver	replica	illusion	navigable	monorail

1. animated
2. fantasy
3. formidable
4. illusion
5. ingenious

6. maneuver
7. menacing
8. monorail
9. navigable
10. replica

WHAT DO THE WORDS MEAN?

>>>> *Following are some meanings, or definitions, for the ten vocabulary words in this lesson. Write the words next to their definitions.*

1. menacing   dangerous; threatening

2. ingenious   showing great originality and cleverness

3. monorail   a kind of train that rides on only one track

4. animated   moving as if alive

5. illusion   a kind of trick that makes something look like it really exists

6. formidable   causing wonder or amazement because of size or greatness

7. replica   a copy

8. maneuver   to direct or guide with skill

9. fantasy   make-believe; imagination

10. navigable   wide and deep enough for travel by boat

COMPLETE THE SENTENCES

>>>> *Use the vocabulary words in this lesson to complete the following sentences. Use each word only once.*

menacing	ingenious	formidable	animated	fantasy
maneuver	replica	illusion	navigable	monorail

1. The Bengal tiger in this zoo looks very ___menacing___.

2. Mickey Mouse is an imaginary character that appears in ___animated___ cartoons.

3. In Walt Disney World's Haunted Mansion, you may think you are seeing a ghost, but it is really only an ___illusion___.

4. Tourists find it difficult to ___maneuver___ their racing cars at high speeds.

5. Because of its size, an elephant is a ___formidable___ animal.

6. Even though the waterways and lakes in Walt Disney World are artificial, they are all ___navigable___.

7. The monorail is an ___ingenious___ invention.

8. It is not easy to make a ___replica___ of atown that no longer exists.

9. People need to escape from the world of reality to one of ___fantasy___.

10. The ___monorail___ is a train that glides on a single overhead track.

USE YOUR OWN WORDS

>>>> *Look at the picture. What words come into your mind? Write them on the lines below. To help you get started, here are two good words:*

1. ___street___
2. ___buildings___
3. ___Answers will vary.___
4. _____
5. _____
6. _____
7. _____
8. _____
9. _____
10. _____

MAKE NEW WORDS FROM OLD

>>>> *Look at the vocabulary word formidable. See how many words you can form by using the letters of this word. Make up at least ten words. Write your words in the spaces below.*

formidable

1. _____ dial _____
2. _____ able _____
3. _____ farm _____
4. _____ roam _____
5. _____ more _____
6. _____ dime _____

7. _____ frame _____
8. _____ blame _____
9. _____ dorm _____
10. _____ marble _____
11. _____ fable _____
12. _____ bride _____

COMPLETE THE STORY

>>>> Here are the ten vocabulary words for this lesson:

animated	menacing	ingenious	fantasy	monorail
maneuver	illusion	navigable	formidable	replica

>>>> *There are six blank spaces in the story below. Four vocabulary words have already been used in the story. They are underlined. Use the other six words to fill in the blanks.*

Mickey Mouse is a well-known little fellow. Walt Disney created many _____ animated _____ cartoons about Mickey and his friends that are enjoyed by children all over the world. Mickey is truly an unusual mouse. He helps his friends when a _____ menacing _____ enemy is about to snatch them up. He can _____ maneuver _____ a ship through <u>navigable</u> water. For a little mouse, he certainly performs some <u>formidable</u> tasks! It would not be surprising even to see him riding a _____ monorail _____ in search of a new adventure.

Surely, Mickey is not an exact _____ replica _____ of a real mouse. He lives in a world of _____ fantasy _____ where mice can think and talk. But to many children, this special mouse is very real, not just an <u>illusion</u>. Children and adults alike owe many hours of entertainment to Walt Disney, the <u>ingenious</u> man who created Mickey more than 50 years ago.

Learn More About Disney Magic

>>>> *On a separate sheet of paper or in your notebook or journal, complete one or more of the activities below.*

Building Language

Imagine you are a consultant in charge of making Walt Disney World understandable to people who speak your native language, not English. Create a plan to help make Disney World an entertaining experience for people who speak your native language.

Broadening Your Understanding

In 1994, business leaders proposed building a new park in Virginia. It was to be a history park, set among the country's historical battlefields. The planned park created huge arguments in Virginia. Some said it was a good way to bring in jobs and tourists and to introduce people to history. Others said that the park would make history into a fairy tale with a happy ending. Think about the arguments for and against a Disney theme park devoted to history. Write a letter to the editor of a Richmond, Virginia, newspaper that will convince others of your position.

Learning Across the Curriculum

Read about the science of animation. Then prepare a picture book for children that explains how animators make Mickey Mouse move on the screen.

4 SHARK!

Swoosh! The shark flaps its powerful tail and propels itself through the water. Its mouth is filled with long, sharp teeth. This is the ruthless great white shark, also known as the man-eater.

An underwater photographer watches the mighty shark. He knows that if the shark sees him, it could overpower him in a matter of seconds. A quick movement might frighten or provoke the shark to attack. Slowly, the photographer backs away. He knows that the situation is fraught with danger.

Suddenly, the shark stops. It sees the photographer and, for a second, seems to scrutinize him carefully. Then it swerves to one side and swims off in another direction. What a close call!

Certainly, this scuba diver was lucky to get out of the water unharmed. After all, the shark is a frightening predator. Some people think that sharks are always hungry. They believe that as soon as sharks finish eating, they are ravenous again. Actually, sharks can go for long periods of time without eating.

Most sharks feed only on small fish. Some follow ships for days to get the food that is thrown overboard. The whale shark, which is sometimes more than 50 feet long, eats only small sea animals and plants.

The white shark and the blue shark are two types of fish that people should be afraid to encounter. Unlike most others, these sharks have been known to attack human beings.

UNDERSTANDING THE STORY

>>>> *Circle the letter next to each correct statement.*

1. The statement that best expresses the main idea of this selection is:
    a. The white shark and the blue shark are the most dangerous sharks.
    b. Sharks are dangerous predators, but most of them feed on small fish rather than humans.
    c. Underwater photographers are often hurt while trying to photograph sharks.

2. From this story, you can conclude that
    a. sharks will disappear as people begin fishing the oceans of the world.
    b. a scuba diver would not be able to overpower a blue shark.
    c. the white shark eats more than any other shark.

MAKE AN ALPHABETICAL LIST

>>>> *Here are the ten vocabulary words in this lesson. Write them in alphabetical order in the spaces below.*

scrutinize	encounter	fraught	ravenous	ruthless
predator	propels	swerves	overpower	provoke

1. encounter
2. fraught
3. overpower
4. predator
5. propels

6. provoke
7. ravenous
8. ruthless
9. scrutinize
10. swerves

WHAT DO THE WORDS MEAN?

>>>> *Following are some meanings, or definitions, for the ten vocabulary words in this lesson. Write the words next to their definitions.*

1. scrutinize — to look at closely; to examine
2. overpower — to defeat because of greater strength; to get the better of by force or power
3. ruthless — showing no mercy or pity
4. propels — pushes forward
5. swerves — moves off a straight course; turns aside
6. fraught — accompanied by; full of
7. provoke — to bring on an action
8. predator — an animal that kills other animals for food
9. encounter — to meet face to face
10. ravenous — very hungry

>>>> *Use the vocabulary words in this lesson to complete the following sentences. Use each word only once.*

scrutinize	encounter	fraught	ravenous	ruthless
predator	propels	swerves	overpower	provoke

1. Sharks will carefully _____scrutinize_____ anyone near them in the water.

2. Divers who _____encounter_____ sharks are often very frightened.

3. The great white shark is the most dangerous _____predator_____ in the sea.

4. Diving in shark-infested water is _____fraught_____ with danger.

5. Although sharks can eat large amounts of food, they do not always have _____ravenous_____ appetites.

6. Notice how quickly the shark _____swerves_____ to one side and disappears behind the coral reef.

7. A diver should not _____provoke_____, or anger, any shark.

8. These huge fish are so strong that they can _____overpower_____ any swimmer.

9. The white shark's huge tail _____propels_____ it through the water.

10. Sailors who are shipwrecked in shark-infested waters fear the sudden appearance of these _____ruthless_____ creatures.

>>>> *Look at the picture. What words come into your mind? Write them on the lines below. To help you get started, here are two good words:*

1. _____water_____
2. _____hand_____
3. ____Answers will vary.____
4. _____
5. _____
6. _____
7. _____
8. _____
9. _____
10. _____

DO THE CROSSWORD PUZZLE

>>>> *In a crossword puzzle, there is a group of boxes, some with numbers in them. There are also two columns of words or definitions, one for "Across" and the other for "Down." Do the puzzle. Each of the words in the puzzle will be one of the vocabulary words in this lesson.*

Across

4. to meet

5. full of

6. moves to one side

7. very hungry

Down

1. to defeat

2. to examine

3. without mercy

						¹o	
²s		³r				v	
⁴e	n	c	o	u	n	t	e	r
r		t				r	
⁵f	r	a	u	g	h	t		p
t		u		l		o	
i				e		w	
n				s		e	
i			⁶s	w	e	r	v	e	s
z						
⁷r	a	v	e	n	o	u	s

COMPLETE THE STORY

>>>> Here are the ten vocabulary words for this lesson:

swerves	fraught	ruthless	propels	overpower
encounter	ravenous	predator	scrutinize	provoke

>>>> *There are six blank spaces in the story below. Four vocabulary words have already been used in the story. They are underlined. Use the other six words to fill in the blanks.*

You are a scuba diver exploring the ocean. The scene around you is <u>fraught</u> with beauty. A small fish swims up to your face. It stops to ____scrutinize____ you carefully and then <u>swerves</u> off in another direction. You are amazed at how its small body ____propels____ itself through the water.

You see a larger fish in the distance. As it comes closer, you see that it is a powerful shark. You are frightened. The last thing you expected was to ____encounter____ a dangerous shark. You know that if you <u>provoke</u> this fish it could ____overpower____ you in seconds. A shark can be a ____ruthless____ <u>predator</u>. If it is really ____ravenous____, it will attack anything it sees—including you! The shark moves off in another direction. That was a close call!

24

Learn More About Sharks

>>>> *On a separate sheet of paper or in your notebook or journal, complete one or more of the activities below.*

Learning Across the Curriculum

There are many kinds of sharks. Research some of these sharks and where they live. Then draw a map of the world's oceans and mark where these different sharks are found.

Broadening Your Understanding

Sharks have a reputation for attacking humans. Research the sharks that have been known to prey on people. Decide which shark you would least like to meet, then imagine you are scuba diving and have just spotted one. Write a fictional account of what happens next.

Extending Your Reading

Sharks have been the subject of horror movies and books. Read one of the following books and decide how realistic the author's writing is about the shark. Defend what you decide in an essay.

White Shark, by Peter Benchley
Jaws, by Deborah Crisfield

The two wrestlers face each other from their corners of the ring. They wear heavy silk belts strapped around their waists. Each wrestler takes a mouthful of water and spits it out. The water is thought to give the wrestlers power.

Then the wrestlers scoop up salt and throw it across the floor. Salt throwing is believed to be an act of *purification.* The men clap their hands and stare at each other in *contempt.* They *disperse* more salt across the floor. Each of these actions is part of the *ritual* of one of Japan's most popular sports—sumo wrestling.

The two wrestlers meet in the center of the ring. Each man weighs more than 300 pounds. The match is over when one of these *titanic* wrestlers forces the other out of the ring or makes him touch the floor with any part of his body other than his feet. Most sumo wrestlers are powerful and *obstinate.* There are two basic *strategies* that are used. Some wrestlers slap, trip, and shove, while others try to grab their opponents by the belt and flip them out of the ring. It is not unusual for a *vanquished* wrestler to find himself in the audience just seconds after the start of a match.

In sumo wrestling, the most *enviable* position is the rank of *yokozuna,* or grand champion. This title is given by the Japanese Sumo Association to wrestlers who really *excel* in the sport. Even though very few are selected, every sumo wrestler dreams of becoming a *yokozuna.* The few who make it are kings in the world of sumo wrestling.

UNDERSTANDING THE STORY

>>>> *Circle the letter next to each correct statement.*

1. The statement that best expresses the main idea of this selection is:
   a. Sumo wrestlers retire early because of all their injuries.
   b. The art of sumo wrestling pits two large, skilled men against each other in a difficult, interesting combat.
   c. Some sumo wrestlers are more stubborn and powerful than others.

2. From this story, you can conclude that
   a. newer strategies for winning will be invented to make sumo wrestling more interesting.
   b. those sumo wrestlers who win the title of *yokozuna,* or grand champion, will be rewarded by gaining fame and fortune.
   c. sumo wrestling will soon be outlawed because it is too violent.

MAKE AN ALPHABETICAL LIST

>>>> *Here are the ten vocabulary words in this lesson. Write them in alphabetical order in the spaces below.*

ritual	excel	titanic	enviable	purification
vanquished	contempt	disperse	strategies	obstinate

1. contempt
2. disperse
3. enviable
4. excel
5. obstinate

6. purification
7. ritual
8. strategies
9. titanic
10. vanquished

WHAT DO THE WORDS MEAN?

>>>> *Following are some meanings, or definitions, for the ten vocabulary words in this lesson. Write the words next to their definitions.*

1. obstinate — stubborn; set in one's ways

2. contempt — a feeling of dislike; having no respect or concern for another

3. titanic — very big and powerful

4. excel — to be better than others; to be superior

5. ritual — a ceremony; an act done in a precise manner according to certain rules

6. disperse — to scatter; to spread

7. enviable — highly desirable; wanted by others

8. strategies — careful or clever plans to reach a goal

9. purification — a cleansing; an act of removing anything that is improper, corrupt, or damaging

10. vanquished — defeated

>>>> *Use the vocabulary words in this lesson to complete the following sentences. Use each word only once.*

ritual	excel	titanic	enviable	purification
vanquished	contempt	disperse	strategies	obstinate

1. A sumo wrestler who desires to become the grand champion must _____excel_____.

2. The wrestlers glare at each other in _____contempt_____.

3. Being a sumo champion is an _____enviable_____ position for any wrestler.

4. Compared to the ordinary Japanese male, the sumo wrestler is _____titanic_____.

5. Sumo wrestlers use different _____strategies_____ to beat their opponents.

6. It may be hard to _____disperse_____ the crowd after an exciting match.

7. When these wrestlers throw salt across the ring, it is considered an act of _____purification_____.

8. The present sumo grand champion _____vanquished_____ many other wrestlers.

9. He was so _____obstinate_____ that he refused to try any new training method.

10. Part of the _____ritual_____ of each match is that the wrestlers try to make each other angry.

USE YOUR OWN WORDS

>>>> *Look at the picture. What words come into your mind? Write them on the lines below. To help you get started, here are two good words:*

1. _____dirt_____
2. _____audience_____
3. _____Answers will vary._____
4. _____
5. _____
6. _____
7. _____
8. _____
9. _____
10. _____

FIND THE ANTONYMS

>>>> **Antonyms** are words that are opposite in meaning. For example, *good* and *bad* and *fast* and *slow* are antonyms.

>>>> *Here are antonyms for six of the vocabulary words. See if you can find the vocabulary words and write them in the spaces on the left.*

	Vocabulary Word	Antonyms
1.	contempt	respect
2.	titanic	small
3.	obstinate	agreeable
4.	enviable	unwanted
5.	vanquished	victorious
6.	purification	dirtying

COMPLETE THE STORY

>>>> Here are the ten vocabulary words for this lesson:

enviable	disperse	ritual	contempt	excel
titanic	strategies	vanquished	obstinate	purification

>>>> *There are six blank spaces in the story below. Four vocabulary words have already been used in the story. They are underlined. Use the other six words to fill in the blanks.*

Sumo wrestling is thousands of years old. Much of the ancient _____ritual_____, such as salt throwing, remains an important part of the sport. When the wrestlers _____disperse_____ this salt, they are taking part in an act of <u>purification</u>. Each wrestler prepares himself for the competition in this way. Even the looks of _____contempt_____ are part of the preparation.

Once the match begins, the <u>titanic</u> wrestlers usually select one of two popular _____strategies_____ to defeat their opponent. Once they choose this method, they are <u>obstinate</u> in their moves and will attempt to control the match. At the end of the match, the _____vanquished_____ wrestler might find himself in the lap of a surprised spectator. The player who is really able to <u>excel</u> in sumo has a chance to become a grand champion. This position is the most _____enviable_____ one of all.

Learn More About Japan

>>>> *On a separate sheet of paper or in your notebook or journal, complete one or more of the activities below.*

Working Together

Ritual is a part of many of Japan's traditional arts, including Nō, a centuries-old form of theater in Japan. Find out more about it by reading a Nō play and performing the play, or part of it, with your group. Before the performance, explain to your audience a little about the background of Nō plays.

Learning Across the Curriculum

Japanese landscape painting has a unique flavor. Find some examples of this landscape painting and some photographs of rural Japan. Then write a short essay about why Japanese landscape painting may have developed the way it did.

Broadening Your Understanding

An American caused shock waves in 1992 when he became the first non-Japanese to become a high-level sumo wrestler. Find out more about Konishiki and the controversy surrounding him. Write a short newspaper article about what you discover.

31

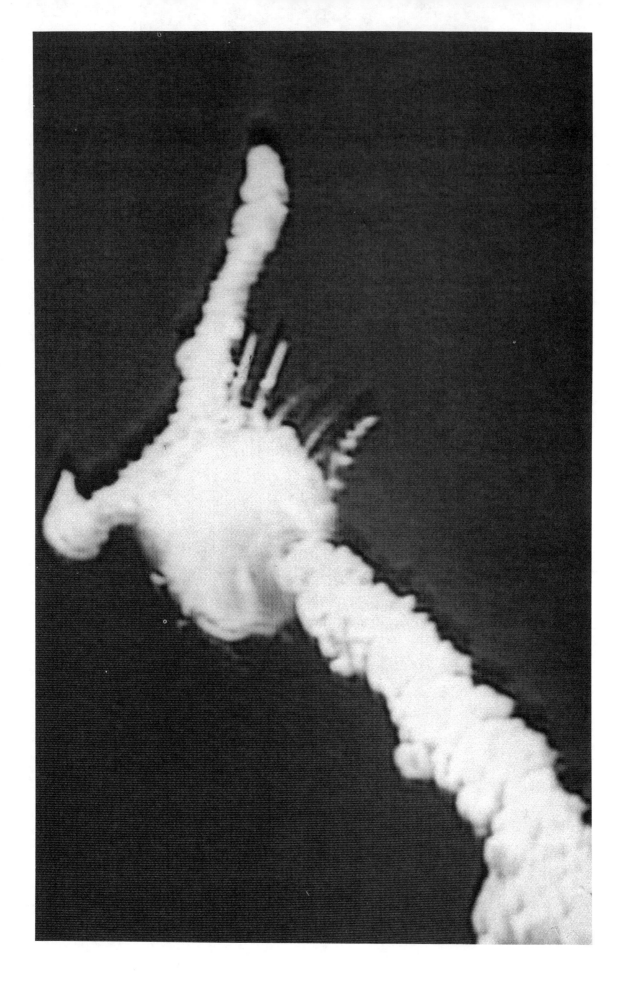

6 SPACE DISASTER

When *Challenger* roared off its launch pad at 11:38 A.M. on January 28, 1986, one crew member was Christa McAuliffe. Chosen by NASA to be the first teacher in space, she planned to broadcast lessons from the shuttle into classrooms across the nation. McAuliffe had no *prior* shuttle experience, but she intended to "humanize the technology of the Space Age." She accomplished her goal, but not in the way she—or anyone else—had planned.

Before the launch, as each step in the *precise* launch *sequence* was checked off, NASA engineers worried about how the day's cold weather might affect the shuttle's *sensitive* systems. Other people were concerned about the public's *reaction* if the flight was canceled. After one delay, the signal was given to go ahead.

Seconds after lift-off, a *defective* joint failed on one of the shuttle's solid-fuel rocket boosters. At 72 seconds into the flight, a spurt of flame from the failed joint *ignited* a fuel tank. Eight miles above the Atlantic Ocean, *Challenger* exploded.

The unthinkable had occurred, and the nation was stunned. The *investment* in *Challenger* had reached far beyond the millions of dollars put into the shuttle itself. Seven lives had been lost. The disaster *tarnished* NASA's image and shook public confidence in the space program. It also taught the lesson that engineers, not *politicians,* must decide whether to proceed with a launch.

The next shuttle wasn't launched until September 1988, after more research and development. Since then, many shuttles have safely orbited Earth, gathering information and adding to our knowledge of the universe. Still, we will not forget the brave crew of *Challenger*.

UNDERSTANDING THE STORY

>>>> *Circle the letter next to each correct statement.*

1. The statement that best expresses the main idea of this selection is:
   a. The explosion of *Challenger* set back the U.S. space program but resulted in many important changes.
   b. It is very risky to fly on shuttle missions.
   c. Launching a shuttle involves a good deal of guessing.

2. From this story, you can conclude that
   a. the crew caused the explosion of *Challenger*.
   b. there will be no more teachers on space shuttles.
   c. design changes have made travel on shuttles much safer.

MAKE AN ALPHABETICAL LIST

>>>> *Here are the ten vocabulary words in this lesson. Write them in alphabetical order in the spaces below.*

politicians	ignited	tarnished	precise	investment
defective	sequence	prior	reaction	sensitive

1. defective

2. ignited

3. investment

4. politicians

5. precise

6. prior

7. reaction

8. sensitive

9. sequence

10. tarnished

WHAT DO THE WORDS MEAN?

>>>> *Following are some meanings, or definitions, for the ten vocabulary words in this lesson. Write the words next to their definitions.*

1. politicians — people who conduct the business of government

2. precise — exact

3. tarnished — made dirty; stained

4. ignited — set on fire

5. defective — faulty; lacking something essential

6. investment — giving something, such as money, in hopes of getting back something valuable

7. prior — earlier; before

8. sequence — items in a certain order

9. reaction — a response to something

10. sensitive — delicate; easily damaged

COMPLETE THE SENTENCES

>>>> *Use the vocabulary words in this lesson to complete the following sentences. Use each word only once.*

sequence	precise	tarnished	prior	sensitive
defective	investment	ignited	reaction	politicians

1. No one seemed to realize that parts of the shuttle were ___defective___.

2. The steps in a shuttle launch must be followed in a ___precise___ order.

3. The engineers did not want to change the ___sequence___ of steps.

4. They worried that the shuttle systems might be ___sensitive___ to cold weather.

5. An unexpected ___reaction___ to cold temperatures could put the mission at risk.

6. The worst possible situation happened when the fuel tank ___ignited___.

7. NASA's record of accomplishments was ___tarnished___ by the disaster.

8. The shuttle represented an ___investment___ of both money and lives.

9. NASA engineers and the ___politicians___ who influenced the decision to launch shared blame for the tragedy.

10. NASA had had many ___prior___ successes before *Challenger* exploded.

USE YOUR OWN WORDS

>>>> *Look at the picture. What words come into your mind? Write them on the lines below. To help you get started, here are two good words:*

1. ___explosion___
2. ___smoke___
3. ___Answers will vary.___
4. _____
5. _____
6. _____
7. _____
8. _____
9. _____
10. _____

MAKE POSSESSIVE WORDS

>>>> The **singular possessive** of a word shows that something belongs to it. For example, Bill has a boat, so it is *Bill's* boat. To make a singular word possessive, add an apostrophe and an *s* to the word, such as *baker's* bread or *class's* teacher. To make a plural word that ends in *s* possessive, add an apostrophe only, such as *friends'* bicycles or *ladies'* hats. To make a plural word that does not end in *s* possessive, add an apostrophe and an *s*, such as *children's* toys.

>>>> *Here are ten words from the story. In the space next to the word, write the correct possessive of the word.*

1. politicians _____politicians'_____   6. crew _____crew's_____
2. NASA _____NASA's_____   7. Earth _____Earth's_____
3. boosters _____boosters'_____   8. *Challenger* _____*Challenger's*_____
4. Christa _____Christa's_____   9. engineers _____engineers'_____
5. public _____public's_____   10. shuttles _____shuttles'_____

COMPLETE THE STORY

>>>> Here are the ten vocabulary words for this lesson:

prior	tarnished	sensitive	investment	defective
reaction	precise	ignited	politicians	sequence

>>>> *There are six blank spaces in the story below. Four vocabulary words have already been used in the story. They are underlined. Use the other six words to fill in the blanks.*

The launch of the *Challenger* required a <u>precise</u> _____sequence_____ of steps. The engineers followed these steps, but they did not realize that certain joints on the shuttle were _____defective_____. They were shocked when the failure of a joint caused a fuel tank to be _____ignited_____.

Public <u>reaction</u> to the tragedy proved that everyone realized the shuttle was an _____investment_____ of both money and lives. <u>Politicians</u> promised action and pointed to many _____prior_____ successes in the space program. NASA was <u>sensitive</u> to the fact that its image had been _____tarnished_____ by the disaster. Since then, many impressive accomplishments have helped to rebuild NASA's reputation.

Learn More About Space Shuttles

>>>> *On a separate sheet of paper or in your notebook or journal, complete one or more of the activities below.*

Learning Across the Curriculum

Write a report describing at least one way the space shuttle missions have contributed to our lives. For example, what have scientists learned from studying living organisms that were brought on board the shuttles? How have foods or fabrics that were developed for space flight helped people on Earth?

Learning Across the Curriculum

Research the background and training of one member of the *Challenger* crew. In addition to Christa McAuliffe, the crew included Dick Scobee, Mike Smith, Judy Resnik, Ellison Onizuka, Ron McNair, and Greg Jarvis. Be sure to find out what motivated the person you chose to fly on *Challenger*.

Broadening Your Understanding

Write an essay explaining whether you would or would not like to fly in a space shuttle, either now or when you are older. Give specific reasons for your choice.

What is the roughest, toughest sport in the world? Some people might argue that it is football. Others might $\boxed{assert}$ that it is hockey. But people who have been to the Asian country of Afghanistan know the answer for sure. For speed, power, and violence, no sport in the world is $\boxed{comparable}$ to the Afghan game of $\boxed{buzkashi}$ (buz-*KA*-shee).

The rules are simple. Two teams of robust men on horses meet on a grassy field. The riders are $\boxed{garbed}$ in colorful costumes.

Suddenly trumpets blare, and a 120-pound goat $\boxed{carcass}$ is thrown to the ground. The game begins. An $\boxed{aggressive}$ rider will snatch up the carcass and gallop off to two distant poles. He must circle each of the poles, race to a circle marked on the ground, and throw the goat into the circle.

His $\boxed{adversaries}$ will do anything they can to stop him. They kick, punch, and shove each other in an attempt to steal the carcass. For a while, it is a $\boxed{gruesome}$ battle of wits, strength, and nerve.

If another player manages to grab the carcass, he then becomes the target for all the other players. Because he is holding the goat, this player is not able to fight back. He cannot even hold the reins of his horse. His horse's speed and his own $\boxed{stamina}$ are his only weapons of defense.

Finally, one $\boxed{dauntless}$ player will break from the confusion and stay clear of the pack. He will circle the poles and reach the circled goal. He will be a hero for having won the roughest game in the world.

UNDERSTANDING THE STORY

>>>> *Circle the letter next to each correct statement.*

1. The statement that best expresses the main idea of this selection is:
   a. There are many similarities between *buzkashi* and football.
   b. The object of *buzkashi* is to throw a goat into the center of a marked circle.
   c. *Buzkashi* may be the most violent sport in the world.

2. From this story, you can conclude that
   a. the excitement of the game outweighs the pain players suffer.
   b. *buzkashi* will soon be popular in other countries.
   c. players of *buzkashi* will decide to wear padding once they see football uniforms.

39

MAKE AN ALPHABETICAL LIST

>>>> *Here are the ten vocabulary words in this lesson. Write them in alphabetical order in the spaces below.*

garbed	stamina	dauntless	aggressive	comparable
gruesome	adversaries	assert	robust	carcass

1. adversaries
2. aggressive
3. assert
4. carcass
5. comparable

6. dauntless
7. garbed
8. gruesome
9. robust
10. stamina

WHAT DO THE WORDS MEAN?

>>>> *Following are some meanings, or definitions, for the ten vocabulary words in this lesson. Write the words next to their definitions.*

1. carcass — a dead body
2. assert — to declare; to state positively
3. comparable — similar; alike in some ways
4. aggressive — showing energy, ambition, and confidence
5. garbed — covered with clothing; dressed
6. robust — strong and healthy
7. gruesome — frightening and ugly
8. adversaries — opponents; enemies
9. stamina — strength; ability to bear fatigue or pain
10. dauntless — brave

COMPLETE THE SENTENCES

>>>> *Use the vocabulary words in this lesson to complete the following sentences. Use each word only once.*

garbed	stamina	dauntless	aggressive	comparable
gruesome	adversaries	assert	robust	carcass

1. *Buzkashi* players must have ___stamina___ in order to last the whole game.

2. A player must be ___aggressive___ and actually grab the carcass out of the hands of another.

3. Only ___robust___ people can play *buzkashi*.

4. Even football is not ___comparable___ to *buzkashi* in terms of violence.

5. Players are ___garbed___ in high boots, long shirts, and baggy pants.

6. The goat ___carcass___ is very heavy and must be held tightly.

7. The number of injuries makes *buzkashi* a ___gruesome___ sport.

8. People respect the player who is ___dauntless___ and daring.

9. Some people ___assert___ that *buzkashi* is the most exciting game in the world.

10. After a game, those who were ___adversaries___ are friends again.

USE YOUR OWN WORDS

>>>> *Look at the picture. What words come into your mind? Write them on the lines below. To help you get started, here are two good words:*

1. ___tail___
2. ___field___
3. ___Answers will vary.___
4. _____
5. _____
6. _____
7. _____
8. _____
9. _____
10. _____

FIND THE ANTONYMS

>>>> **Antonyms** are words that are opposite in meaning. For example, *good* and *bad* and *heavy* and *light* are antonyms.

>>>> *Here are antonyms for six of the vocabulary words. See if you can find the vocabulary words and write them in the spaces on the left.*

	Vocabulary Words	Antonyms
1.	assert	deny
2.	stamina	weakness
3.	adversaries	allies
4.	dauntless	timid
5.	garbed	unclothed
6.	comparable	different

COMPLETE THE STORY

>>>> Here are the ten vocabulary words for this lesson:

gruesome	carcass	comparable	stamina	robust
garbed	adversaries	dauntless	aggressive	assert

>>>> *There are six blank spaces in the story below. Four vocabulary words have already been used in the story. They are underlined. Use the other six words to fill in the blanks.*

As you sit on your horse waiting for the game to begin, you wonder whether you will have the _____ stamina _____ to play well. Your _____ adversaries _____ are all robust men, eager to show their strength and skill. They are _____ garbed _____ in bright costumes. As you wait, you think about being the first to snatch up the goat carcass. It takes an _____ aggressive _____ player to make this first move, but you are eager to be a champion.

Suddenly, the game begins. In a second, a _____ dauntless _____ rider in a wool cap grabs the heavy carcass. The gruesome battle is underway. The air is filled with dust as horses gallop across the field. You charge after the pack of men and horses. You are sure that you agree with those people who _____ assert _____ that no other game in the world is comparable to this Afghan sport called *buzkashi*.

42

Learn More About Rough Sports

>>>> *On a separate sheet of paper or in your notebook or journal, complete one or more of the activities below.*

Building Language

Different sports are popular in different parts of the world. Choose a sport that is popular among people who speak your native language. Then listen to a game broadcast in your native language. Write down the phrases that the announcers use to describe the game or think of the phrases from memory. Translate them into English. On a piece of paper next to each phrase, write what a similar English phrase might be. If you are having trouble thinking of sports phrases in English, have a classmate who is a sports fan help you out.

Learning Across the Curriculum

Many sports that high-school athletes play can be dangerous. Football, wrestling, hockey, and lacrosse are often mentioned as sports in which safety needs to be on the minds of players. Choose one of these sports. Talk to a coach or research ways that athletes participating in this game can play safely. Write a report that includes information about protective equipment, training, and conduct during the game.

Broadening Your Understanding

Boxing is a sport that many love. Others want to ban the sport and say that boxing can injure and even kill participants. Research this sport, including this controversy, and write an argument to either continue boxing or to ban it.

A pilot sees a flashing oval-shaped object flying 500 feet above his airplane. Two other pilots in nearby planes **verify** this report. A radar station locates the object and reports that it is moving at 4,500 miles per hour.

All around the world, people report that they have seen similar objects. Others say that they have seen such sights but have not reported them for fear of public **ridicule.** Still others claim that they have been taken aboard these unusual spaceships.

For years, many **conscientious** scientists have worked hard to explain what are now called UFOs—<u>U</u>nidentified <u>F</u>lying <u>O</u>bjects. According to some, there is **undeniable** proof that UFOs exist. Studies have revealed areas of **scorched** land where people say UFOs have landed. There have been photographs taken that seem to show that these **phenomena** really do exist.

On October 9, 1989, some children in a small Russian town told an amazing UFO story. They reported that a spaceship descended near them. Out of the ship came several 13-foot-tall, headless, three-eyed creatures. The children said one creature pointed a tube at a 16-year-old boy, causing him to vanish. The boy reappeared later.

This story may be difficult to believe, but several Russian scientists took it seriously. Other scientists may **dismiss** some UFO sightings as **optical** illusions. This story makes it clear that it will be difficult to **dispel** the UFO **controversy.**

UNDERSTANDING THE STORY

>>>> *Circle the letter next to each correct statement.*

1. The statement that best expresses the main idea of this selection is:
   a. Areas of scorched land prove without a doubt that UFOs exist.
   b. UFOs cause many problems, including stalled cars.
   c. Some UFOs may really be spaceships from unknown places.

2. From this story, you can conclude that
   a. it will be discovered that UFOs are spaceships from Jupiter.
   b. proving that UFOs are spaceships with visitors from outer space is very difficult.
   c. people who claim to have seen UFOs are just looking for attention.

MAKE AN ALPHABETICAL LIST

>>>> *Here are the ten vocabulary words in this lesson. Write them in alphabetical order in the spaces below.*

scorched	verify	dismiss	conscientious	undeniable
ridicule	dispel	optical	phenomena	controversy

1. conscientious
2. controversy
3. dismiss
4. dispel
5. optical

6. phenomena
7. ridicule
8. scorched
9. undeniable
10. verify

WHAT DO THE WORDS MEAN?

>>>> *Following are some meanings, or definitions, for the ten vocabulary words in this lesson. Write the words next to their definitions.*

1. ridicule — laugh at or make fun of

2. scorched — burned

3. dismiss — to disbelieve; to disregard

4. optical — having to do with vision or the eyes

5. dispel — to clear away

6. conscientious — thoughtful; careful

7. controversy — cause of disagreement or argument

8. verify — to agree or prove that something is true

9. phenomena — something that strikes people as strange or uncommon; a visible appearance

10. undeniable — plainly true; not questionable

COMPLETE THE SENTENCES

>>>> *Use the vocabulary words in this lesson to complete the following sentences. Use each word only once.*

scorched	verify	dismiss	conscientious	undeniable
ridicule	dispel	optical	phenomena	controversy

1. The _____controversy_____ over UFOs has raged since the first report of a sighting in 1947.

2. There is no _____undeniable_____ proof that UFOs do or do not exist.

3. Scientists cannot _____dismiss_____ all sightings of UFOs.

4. Shooting stars are _____phenomena_____ that might be mistaken for UFOs.

5. Like mirages in deserts, UFOs may be _____optical_____ illusions.

6. It is impossible to _____verify_____ that a photograph is of a UFO.

7. _____Conscientious_____ scientists have tried to check out every detail of UFO reports.

8. To avoid _____ridicule_____, most people will not report seeing UFOs.

9. They seek other explanations that will _____dispel_____ the idea of UFOs.

10. But what, other than a UFO, could have _____scorched_____ the grass like this?

USE YOUR OWN WORDS

>>>> *Look at the picture. What words come into your mind? Write them on the lines below. To help you get started, here are two good words:*

1. _____house_____
2. _____trees_____
3. ___Answers will vary.___
4. _____
5. _____
6. _____
7. _____
8. _____
9. _____
10. _____

FIND THE ANALOGIES

>>>> In an **analogy,** similar relationships occur between words that are different. For example, *pig* is to *hog* as *car* is to *automobile*. The relationship is that the words have the same meaning. Here's another analogy: *noisy* is to *quiet* as *short* is to *tall*. In this relationship, the words have opposite meanings.

>>>> *See if you can complete the following analogies. Circle the correct word or words.*

1. **Dismiss** is to **reject** as **dispel** is to
   a. attract   **b.** scatter   **c.** gather   **d.** send

2. **Scorched** is to **burned** as **drenched** is to
   a. soaked   **b.** dry   **c.** thirsty   **d.** hot

3. **Verify** is to **prove** as **prevent** is to
   a. ask   **b.** help   **c.** allow   **d.** block

4. **Controversy** is to **argument** as **ridicule** is to
   a. happiness   **b.** laughter   **c.** disagreement   **d.** anger

5. **Undeniable** is to **questionable** as **honest** is to
   a. smart   **b.** quiet   **c.** untruthful   **d.** mean

COMPLETE THE STORY

>>>> Here are the ten vocabulary words for this lesson:

controversy	ridicule	verify	scorched	optical
dispel	undeniable	dismiss	phenomena	conscientious

>>>> *There are six blank spaces in the story below. Four vocabulary words have already been used in the story. They are underlined. Use the other six words to fill in the blanks.*

When the U.S. Air Force study of UFOs became available to the public, many people hoped they could _____dispel_____ all doubts about UFOs. Although the study stated that many UFO sightings were only <u>optical</u> illusions, the _____controversy_____ continues.

After all, the photographs of these _____phenomena_____ seem to offer <u>undeniable</u> proof that UFOs are more than illusions. What about the areas of _____scorched_____ earth where witnesses claim that the sophisticated flying machines have landed? These witnesses give _____conscientious_____ thought to their reports. They know they could become the subject of jokes and public <u>ridicule</u>. But these people are sure we have all the facts we need to _____verify_____ the existence of UFOs. They refuse to <u>dismiss</u> the sightings.

48

Learn More About the Universe

>>>> *On a separate sheet of paper or in your notebook or journal, complete one or more of the activities below.*

Learning Across the Curriculum

In 1992, the federal space agency NASA stepped up its search for life in outer space using SETI. Use newspaper and magazine articles to find out what SETI is and how NASA hopes to use it to find out if there is life on other planets.

Broadening Your Understanding

H. G. Wells's book *The War of the Worlds* was produced as a radio drama in 1938. The broadcast was so realistic that it caused a panic among thousands who thought Earth was under attack by people from another planet. Research this event and then write an essay explaining whether you think it would or would not be possible to fool people in the same way today.

Extending Your Reading

Do UFOs really exist? Read one of these books and write an essay about whether the book convinced you one way or the other. Justify your opinion.

Are There Alien Beings? by Gerald S. Snyder
Aliens and UFOs: Messengers or Deceivers? by James L. Thompson
U.F.O.s, by Robert Jackson
Unidentified Flying Objects, by Isaac Asimov

9 PALACE OF PRIDE

When the empress of India died in 1631, her **bereaved** husband built a memorial to honor her. The building of this memorial was a **laborious** task. More than 20,000 men worked for over 20 years to complete it. It was made of white marble with a **massive** dome that is 120 feet high. The name of the building came from the title of the empress, Mumtaz-i-Mahal, which means "pride of the palace." It is called the Taj Mahal.

The Taj Mahal may well be the loveliest building in India. It rests on an **octagonal** platform of red stone. Four slender prayer towers stand at each corner of the platform. In front of the building is a garden of clipped bushes and **rectangular** pools. These pools reflect the image of the building with its rounded dome and graceful curves. The outer walls of the Taj Mahal are decorated with many **inscriptions** from the Koran, the holy book of Islam.

Inside, a soft light shines on a **magnificent** screen of carved marble. Behind the screen lie two monuments honoring Mumtaz-i-Mahal and her husband, Shah Jahan. The monuments are covered with precious stones from all over the world. The bodies of the **regal** couple are buried below the main floor. They are in an underground **crypt.**

Hundreds of years after his death, Shah Jahan is still remembered as the man who built the Taj Mahal. This **exquisite** memorial is famous not only for its beauty but also because it was built with more than marble and stone. It was built with love.

UNDERSTANDING THE STORY

>>>> *Circle the letter next to each correct statement.*

1. The statement that best expresses the main idea of this selection is:
   a. It took 20 years to complete the Taj Mahal.
   b. The money, time, and labor spent in building the Taj Mahal were wasteful.
   c. The Taj Mahal is a magnificent memorial honoring the wife of Shah Jahan.

2. From this story, you can conclude that
   a. other emperors will build memorials to their loved ones.
   b. the Taj Mahal will be used for more practical purposes in the future.
   c. the beauty of the Taj Mahal attracts tourists from all over the world.

MAKE AN ALPHABETICAL LIST

>>>> *Here are the ten vocabulary words in this lesson. Write them in alphabetical order in the spaces below.*

inscriptions	rectangular	massive	crypt	regal
magnificent	bereaved	exquisite	octagonal	laborious

1. bereaved
2. crypt
3. exquisite
4. inscriptions
5. laborious

6. magnificent
7. massive
8. octagonal
9. rectangular
10. regal

WHAT DO THE WORDS MEAN?

>>>> *Following are some meanings, or definitions, for the ten vocabulary words in this lesson. Write the words next to their definitions.*

1. crypt — underground vault or chamber

2. exquisite — of exceptional quality, beauty, or detail

3. magnificent — grand; stately; splendid

4. regal — having to do with kings and queens; royal

5. octagonal — having eight sides

6. inscriptions — words that are written or carved in stone to make them last

7. rectangular — having four sides with four right angles

8. laborious — involving or requiring very hard work

9. bereaved — saddened by the death of a loved one; feeling a loss

10. massive — large, solid, or heavy

COMPLETE THE SENTENCES

>>>> *Use the vocabulary words in this lesson to complete the following sentences. Use each word only once.*

inscriptions	rectangular	massive	crypt	regal
magnificent	bereaved	exquisite	octagonal	laborious

1. Few modern buildings are as _____magnificent_____ as the Taj Mahal.

2. _____Inscriptions_____ from the Koran decorate the outer walls of the Taj Mahal.

3. When a building is fit for royalty, it can be described as _____regal_____.

4. The precious stones and art work in the Taj Mahal are _____exquisite_____.

5. Shah Jahan, the _____bereaved_____ husband of the empress, built this stately building to honor her memory.

6. The royal couple is buried beneath the main floor in a _____crypt_____.

7. The _____rectangular_____ shape of the pools adds beauty to the landscape.

8. The white dome on top of the Taj Mahal is _____massive_____ in size.

9. Art critics consider the Taj Mahal's _____octagonal_____ platform unusually attractive.

10. Constructing the Taj Mahal was a lengthy, _____laborious_____ task.

USE YOUR OWN WORDS

>>>> *Look at the picture. What words come into your mind? Write them on the lines below. To help you get started, here are two good words:*

1. _____shrubs_____
2. _____dome_____
3. _____Answers will vary._____
4. _____
5. _____
6. _____
7. _____
8. _____
9. _____
10. _____

FIND THE ANALOGIES

>>>> In an **analogy,** similar relationships occur between words that are different. For example, *pig* is to *hog* as *car* is to *automobile*. The relationship is that the words have the same meaning. Here's another analogy: *noisy* is to *quiet* as *short* is to *tall*. In this relationship, the words have opposite meanings.

>>>> *See if you can complete the following analogies. Circle the correct word or words.*

1. **Rectangular** is to **four-sided** as **octagonal** is to
   a. two-sided   **b.** six-sided   **c.** eight-sided   **d.** twelve-sided

2. **Slender** is to **thin** as **massive** is to
   a. large   **b.** tiny   **c.** light   **d.** many

3. **Magnificent** is to **splendid** as **regal** is to
   a. royal   **b.** brave   **c.** poor   **d.** real

4. **Laborious** is to **easy** as **quick** is to
   a. fast   **b.** difficult   **c.** rushed   **d.** slow

5. **Bereaved** is to **happy** as **exquisite** is to
   a. pretty   **b.** ugly   **c.** sad   **d.** foreign

COMPLETE THE STORY

>>>> Here are the ten vocabulary words for this lesson:

crypt	regal	magnificent	bereaved	exquisite
laborious	rectangular	inscriptions	octagonal	massive

>>>> *There are six blank spaces in the story below. Four vocabulary words have already been used in the story. They are underlined. Use the other six words to fill in the blanks.*

Anyone who visits India will want to see the <u>exquisite</u> Taj Mahal. As you approach the building, you can see it reflected in large _____rectangular_____ pools of water. The slender prayer towers in four corners of the <u>octagonal</u> platform rise above the building. The <u>massive</u> dome shows why it took years of _____laborious_____ effort to build the Taj Mahal. Long hours of work were required to finish the carved _____inscriptions_____ that decorate the walls.

The Taj Mahal was built during a period of great sadness. The _____bereaved_____ Shah Jahan built it in memory of his wife. Today this _____regal_____ couple is buried in a _____crypt_____ under this <u>magnificent</u> palace.

Learn More About Magnificent Monuments

>>>> *On a separate sheet of paper or in your notebook or journal, complete one or more of the activities below.*

Learning Across the Curriculum

The architecture of a country, including its monuments, can be a guide to its history and culture. Research the architecture of a city or a country. Write a short essay explaining why the architecture looks as it does. One good source of information is travel guide books.

Broadening Your Understanding

The Taj Mahal has come to be known as a building that symbolizes India. Think about the famous buildings and monuments of the United States, including the White House, the Washington Monument, the Statue of Liberty, Gettysburg Military Park, and Gettysburg National Cemetery. Which do you think best symbolizes the United States? Why?

Extending Your Reading

Read one of these books about the Vietnam Memorial. Write why you think the monument was so controversial.

The Story of the Vietnam Memorial, by David Wright
Always to Remember, by Brent Ashabranner
The Wall: A Day at the Vietnam Veterans Memorial, by Peter Meyer
The Wall, by Sal Lopes

Bertha Knox Gilkey says she will never forget the old *tenement* building where she lived as a young child. It had a dirt floor and no hot or cold running water. She also remembers being taught that poverty was no excuse for improper behavior. A person was held *accountable* for what he or she did.

When her family moved to Cochran, a housing development in Missouri, they thought they had moved to heaven. But as more and more families moved to Cochran, what was once called Cochran Gardens became just another *neglected* housing project.

While her friends and neighbors moved out or simply accepted the *deterioration* around them, Gilkey was determined to make Cochran succeed. She took the gang leaders and created *renovation* crews. Instead of *vandalizing* the property, these kids now began to restore it. As she said, "We changed the people before we changed the building." She urged all the *tenants* to gain control of their community and their *destiny.*

Bertha Knox Gilkey became president of the Cochran Tenant Management Corporation, where she continued her *crusade* for tenants' rights. She was especially proud of being invited to the White House for the signing of a bill that gave tenants a greater role in managing their homes. After changing the *fabric* of her own community, Gilkey went on to travel throughout the world, encouraging others to join in the fight for personal dignity.

UNDERSTANDING THE STORY

>>>> *Circle the letter next to each correct statement.*

1. The statement that best expresses the main idea of this selection is:
   a. Bertha Knox Gilkey is a crusader for tenants' rights.
   b. Bertha Knox Gilkey is trying to forget about growing up in an old tenement building.
   c. Bertha Knox Gilkey overcame a poor childhood.

2. From this story, you can conclude that
   a. Bertha Knox Gilkey will be invited to the White House next year.
   b. Bertha Knox Gilkey can be very persuasive.
   c. Bertha Knox Gilkey wants to renovate her old tenement building.

MAKE AN ALPHABETICAL LIST

>>>> *Here are the ten vocabulary words in this lesson. Write them in alphabetical order in the spaces below.*

vandalizing	accountable	crusade	fabric	deterioration
tenants	tenement	neglected	renovation	destiny

1. accountable
2. crusade
3. destiny
4. deterioration
5. fabric
6. neglected
7. renovation
8. tenants
9. tenement
10. vandalizing

WHAT DO THE WORDS MEAN?

>>>> *Following are some meanings, or definitions, for the ten vocabulary words in this lesson. Write the words next to their definitions.*

1. neglected — not cared for; left unattended
2. destiny — what happens to someone; fate
3. accountable — responsible; answerable
4. crusade — a strong attempt to promote a cause or an idea
5. tenement — an apartment building
6. fabric — the structure; the quality (of something)
7. tenants — renters; people who occupy property owned by another
8. renovation — the act of repairing something to look like new
9. vandalizing — intentionally damaging or destroying property
10. deterioration — worsening of conditions or value

COMPLETE THE SENTENCES

>>>> *Use the vocabulary words in this lesson to complete the following sentences. Use each word only once.*

tenement	crusade	renovation	deterioration	vandalizing
accountable	destiny	fabric	neglected	tenants

1. Gilkey believes people should have control of their own _____destiny_____.

2. People living in a _____tenement_____ can improve the conditions of their lives.

3. Gilkey urges _____tenants_____ to fight for their rights.

4. She believes that we are all _____accountable_____ for our actions.

5. According to Gilkey, we have the power to improve the _____fabric_____ of our lives.

6. Gilkey is upset when she sees a _____neglected_____ community.

7. Not caring about a building often leads to its _____deterioration_____.

8. Gilkey will not tolerate anyone _____vandalizing_____ her housing development.

9. She devotes her life to a _____crusade_____ for personal dignity.

10. When she sees a decaying building, Gilkey urges _____renovation_____.

USE YOUR OWN WORDS

>>>> *Look at the picture. What words come into your mind? Write them on the lines below. To help you get started, here are two good words:*

1. _____attractive_____
2. _____silky_____
3. ___Answers will vary.___
4. _____
5. _____
6. _____
7. _____
8. _____
9. _____
10. _____

>>>> *Each group of letters represents one of the vocabulary words for this lesson. Can you unscramble them? Write your answers in the blanks on the right.*

1. reacsud   crusade

2. nettneem   tenement

3. carbif   fabric

4. geledcent   neglected

5. lidavignanz   vandalizing

6. tydeins   destiny

7. senttan   tenants

8. onnevitoar   renovation

9. uncoblatace   accountable

10. riodoraniette   deterioration

COMPLETE THE STORY

>>>> Here are the ten vocabulary words for this lesson:

renovation	crusade	neglected	accountable	vandalizing
deterioration	destiny	tenants	fabric	tenement

>>>> *There are six blank spaces in the story below. Four vocabulary words have already been used in the story. They are underlined. Use the other six words to fill in the blanks.*

Bertha Knox Gilkey's life has been one long <u>crusade</u>. She knows what it is like to live in an old _____tenement_____. She uses the lessons she learned as a child to teach others that we are all _____accountable_____ for what we do.

When she saw the <u>deterioration</u> of Cochran, Gilkey knew it was time to fight back. She was offended by young <u>tenants</u> who were _____vandalizing_____ their own buildings. She persuaded them to direct their energy toward _____renovation_____ rather than destruction.

Gilkey will not tolerate people or property being _____neglected_____. Clearly, it is her <u>destiny</u> to improve the _____fabric_____ of life throughout the United States and abroad.

Learn More About Social Problems

>>>> *On a separate sheet of paper or in your notebook or journal, complete one or more of the activities below.*

Building Language

Imagine you are in charge of helping people in your community who speak your native language. What is the most important need of these people? What is the best way to address that need and change things? Write a plan to make your ideas become a reality.

Broadening Your Understanding

Bertha Knox Gilkey is dedicated to tenants' rights. Others have organized to help feed the hungry, house the homeless, educate teenagers, and stop violence in their communities. Choose an area of need in which you are interested. Then find out the opportunities for volunteering in this area in your community. One good source of information is your local United Way. Make a poster outlining the opportunities for volunteering that you have discovered. Hang the poster in your classroom.

Extending Your Reading

Read one of these books about social problems or find a book about a problem in which you are interested. Then write about ways that teenagers can help solve the problem.

The Hunger Road, by John Christopher Fine
Anyplace but Here: Young, Alone, and Homeless, by Ellen Switzer
Famine and Hunger, by Lawrence Williams
No Place to Be: Voices of Homeless Children, by Judith Berck

You are standing in a room below ground. It is cool and dark, but there is *adequate* light for you to look around. Behind you is the narrow *corridor* that led into this room. Ahead of you stands your guide, who has stopped to tell you about this *phenomenal* structure.

"Welcome to the most famous Egyptian *pyramid,*" he begins. "It is called the Great Pyramid. It was built almost 5,000 years ago by a pharaoh, or ruler, named Khufu. Like other rulers, Khufu wanted a tomb where he would be placed after his death. The early Egyptians believed in life after death. So the pharaoh was buried with food, clothing, jewelry, and *sundry* other items. He wanted all of these possessions *accessible* to him in his next life.

"This pyramid is a structure of great *magnitude.* It is more than 450 feet high—as tall as a 40-story *skyscraper.* The bottom is wide enough to cover more than eight football fields. It is made of more than 2 million stone blocks. Each one weighs 2½ tons.

"No one knows exactly how the Great Pyramid was built. Probably, the blocks were floated across the valley to this spot when the Nile River overflowed. One ancient historian says that 100,000 slaves worked for 20 years to complete the job. Considering the magnitude of the pyramid, this estimate is very *plausible.*

"Now, we will follow the corridor to the Chamber of Queens and, *adjacent* to this chamber, the Great Hall. Follow me to see more of the Great Pyramid, one of the Seven Wonders of the World."

UNDERSTANDING THE STORY

>>>> *Circle the letter next to each correct statement.*

1. The statement that best expresses the main idea of this selection is:
   a. It took 100,000 slaves 20 years to complete the Great Pyramid.
   b. This magnificent structure was built to make Khufu comfortable in his life after death.
   c. The pyramids are one of the Seven Wonders of the World.
2. From this story, you can conclude that
   a. modern Egyptians are proud of the huge pyramids that were built by their ancient ancestors.
   b. the money and human power needed to construct the Great Pyramid were wasted.
   c. the historical value of the pyramids is not as great as it used to be.

MAKE AN ALPHABETICAL LIST

>>>> *Here are the ten vocabulary words in this lesson. Write them in alphabetical order in the spaces below.*

| sundry | pyramid | accessible | phenomenal | corridor |
| magnitude | adequate | adjacent | skyscraper | plausible |

1. accessible
2. adequate
3. adjacent
4. corridor
5. magnitude

6. phenomenal
7. plausible
8. pyramid
9. skyscraper
10. sundry

WHAT DO THE WORDS MEAN?

>>>> *Following are some meanings, or definitions, for the ten vocabulary words in this lesson. Write the words next to their definitions.*

1. skyscraper — a very tall building

2. magnitude — size

3. plausible — believable; reasonable

4. pyramid — an ancient structure, made of blocks, with a square bottom and four sides shaped like triangles that meet in a point at the top

5. corridor — a hallway that connects rooms

6. adequate — just enough

7. adjacent — near; connected

8. sundry — various; miscellaneous

9. phenomenal — remarkable; amazing

10. accessible — within reach; easy to get at

COMPLETE THE SENTENCES

>>>> *Use the vocabulary words in this lesson to complete the following sentences. Use each word only once.*

adequate	accessible	phenomenal	magnitude	corridor
skyscraper	pyramid	plausible	sundry	adjacent

1. The light in the Great Pyramid is _____adequate_____ for people to see.

2. The Great Pyramid is a _____phenomenal_____ structure.

3. A _____pyramid_____ is a four-sided structure with sides that rise to a point.

4. Today, the pyramids are _____accessible_____ to tourists visiting Egypt.

5. There is a _____corridor_____ leading from the Great Hall to the Queen's Chamber.

6. The Great Pyramid is almost as tall as a 40-story _____skyscraper_____.

7. The _____magnitude_____ of the Great Pyramid can be understood when we realize that it is more than 450 feet high.

8. When the pharaohs died, the Egyptians made sure that their jewelry, food, and _____sundry_____ other necessities were buried with them.

9. It is _____plausible_____ to assume that the Great Pyramid took many years to build.

10. Usually, the Queen's Chamber was _____adjacent_____ to the King's Chamber, but not in this case.

USE YOUR OWN WORDS

>>>> *Look at the picture. What words come into your mind? Write them on the lines below. To help you get started, here are two good words:*

1. _____road_____
2. _____sand_____
3. _____Answers will vary._____
4. _____
5. _____
6. _____
7. _____
8. _____
9. _____
10. _____

65

FIND THE SUBJECTS AND PREDICATES

>>>> The **subject** of a sentence names the person, place, or thing that is spoken about. The **predicate** of a sentence is what is said about the subject. For example:

> The small boy went to the football game.

>>>> The *small boy* is the subject (the person the sentence is talking about). *Went to the football game* is the predicate of the sentence (because it tells what the small boy did).

>>>> *In the following sentences, draw one line under the subject of the sentence and two lines under the predicate of the sentence.*

1. The guide stops to talk about the pyramid.
2. The Great Pyramid was built almost 5,000 years ago.
3. It is as tall as a 40-story building.
4. The early Egyptians believed in life after death.
5. Each block weighs 2 1/2 tons.

COMPLETE THE STORY

>>>> Here are the ten vocabulary words for this lesson:

accessible	plausible	phenomenal	magnitude	adequate
skyscraper	pyramid	corridor	adjacent	sundry

>>>> *There are six blank spaces in the story below. Four vocabulary words have already been used in the story. They are underlined. Use the other six words to fill in the blanks.*

In the Egyptian desert is one of the most ___phenomenal___ structures ever built. It is a stone ___pyramid___ that was built thousands of years ago by a pharaoh named Khufu. The inside of the Great Pyramid has a long ___corridor___ that leads to rooms that are underlined adjacent to one another. Although there is ___adequate___ light, a visitor must be careful not to get lost. He or she must follow the guide carefully in order to see each of the rooms and the sundry items that were ___accessible___ to the pharaoh after his death.

The Great Pyramid is as tall as a 40-story skyscraper. Because of its great ___magnitude___, it took 20 years to build. It is quite plausible that 100,000 slaves were needed to move the heavy blocks.

Learn More About Ancient Egyptians

>>>> *On a separate sheet of paper or in your notebook or journal, complete one or more of the activities below.*

Learning Across the Curriculum

Discover how ancient Egyptians kept track of the hours in a day and the days in a month or year. Research and demonstrate for the class the Egyptians' ancient water clock or their calendar.

Broadening Your Understanding

The ancient Egyptians are well known for their burial rites. Research how the ancient Egyptians made mummies. Explain the process in an oral presentation.

Extending Your Reading

Read one of these books about Egyptian rulers and their tombs. Then write what you think daily life was like for the kings of ancient Egypt.

Mummies, Tombs and Treasure: Secrets of Ancient Egypt, by Lila Perl
In Search of Tutankhamun, by Piero Ventura and Gian Paolo Ceserani
Tales of a Dead King, by Walter Dean Myers
The Tombs of the Pharaohs, by Sue Clarke

12 YO YO MA

The music teacher was astonished. He had heard cellists play a suite by Johann Sebastian Bach before. But he had never heard a 4-year-old play one! That child was Yo Yo Ma, who grew up to be a world-famous musician.

Ma had learned that difficult piece from his father. Hiao-Tsiun Ma used a teaching technique that might be called "divide and conquer." The first day, his father had Ma memorize only two measures of the suite. The next day, Ma memorized two more. Each day, Ma learned two more measures until he had memorized the entire piece.

Ma later applied this technique to many problems of music, school, and life. He would break a complicated problem into its basic components. It was easier to understand one component at a time. Then he could soon understand the whole problem.

One of Ma's problems was dealing with contradictory cultures. When he was 7 years old, his family moved to America. At home, Yo Yo Ma spoke Chinese and adhered to the traditional values of his heritage. This meant accepting all of his family's values.

Outside the home, however, Ma was immersed in the freer culture of America. He adjusted to this freedom quickly. His teacher saw Ma's need to show his own individuality. He reacted by giving Ma more leeway to experiment with his music.

The teacher had made a wise choice. From that point on, Ma has given fresh, enthusiastic interpretations to some of the world's greatest music.

UNDERSTANDING THE STORY

>>>> *Circle the letter next to each correct statement.*

1. The statement that best expresses the main idea of this selection is:
   a. Parents should not tutor their own children.
   b. Great artists need freedom to be themselves.
   c. It is best to learn to play music at a young age.

2. From this story, you can conclude that
   a. Yo Yo Ma drifted away from his family completely.
   b. Yo Yo Ma stopped taking lessons from other musicians.
   c. Yo Yo Ma encourages all people to find their own individuality.

69

MAKE AN ALPHABETICAL LIST

>>>> *Here are the ten vocabulary words in this lesson. Write them in alphabetical order in the spaces below.*

astonished	suite	technique	individuality	components
contradictory	adhered	leeway	adjusted	immersed

1. adhered
2. adjusted
3. astonished
4. components
5. contradictory

6. immersed
7. individuality
8. leeway
9. suite
10. technique

WHAT DO THE WORDS MEAN?

>>>> *Following are some meanings, or definitions, for the ten vocabulary words in this lesson. Write the words next to their definitions.*

1. suite — a series of musical movements that vary in number and character

2. leeway — convenient room for freedom of action

3. components — necessary parts; the parts that make up the whole

4. technique — a method or skill in doing something

5. immersed — absorbed; involved deeply

6. astonished — amazed; greatly surprised

7. contradictory — opposed; in disagreement with

8. individuality — qualities that make one person different from all others

9. adhered — hold closely; followed

10. adjusted — adapted; got used to

70

COMPLETE THE SENTENCES

>>>> *Use the vocabulary words in this lesson to complete the following sentences. Use each word only once.*

astonished	suite	technique	individuality	components
contradictory	adhered	leeway	adjusted	immersed

1. Yo Yo Ma's father was probably _____astonished_____ by his son's behavior.

2. A _____technique_____ for learning music may be helpful in learning other subjects.

3. The basic _____components_____ in Yo Yo Ma's learning the Bach piece were two-measure sections.

4. The Chinese are not the only people whose children have _____adhered_____ to family values.

5. Some immigrants to this country _____adjusted_____ to its culture more easily than others.

6. A _____suite_____ emphasizes the variety possible in music.

7. Most people begin to express their _____individuality_____ during adolescence.

8. The _____contradictory_____ attitudes between parents and children often show up in matters, such as clothing, music, and personal habits.

9. Giving Yo Yo Ma _____leeway_____ brought out his potential more fully.

10. Few people succeed in an activity unless they have _____immersed_____ themselves in it.

USE YOUR OWN WORDS

>>>> *Look at the picture. What words come into your mind? Write them on the lines below. To help you get started, here are two good words:*

1. _____smile_____
2. _____hands_____
3. ____Answers will vary.____
4. _____
5. _____
6. _____
7. _____
8. _____
9. _____
10. _____

FIND THE ANALOGIES

>>>> In an **analogy,** similar relationships occur between words that are different. For example, *pig* is to *hog* as *car* is to *automobile*. The relationship is that the words have the same meaning. Here's another analogy: *noisy* is to *quiet* as *short* is to *tall*. In this relationship, the words have opposite meanings.

>>>> *See if you can complete the following analogies. Circle the correct word or words.*

1. **Adhere** is to **follow** as **photograph** is to

a. camera   **b.** photographer   **c.** picture   **d.** develop

2. **component** is to **whole** as **slice** is to

a. frightened   **b.** surprised   **c.** pie   **d.** disappointed

3. **Building** is to **structure** as **contradictory** is to

a. similar   **b.** rigid   **c.** agreed   **d.** opposed

4. **Individuality** is to **uniqueness** as **adjust** is to

a. struggle   **b.** adapt   **c.** stick to   **d.** rule

5. **Immerse** is to **involve** as **technique** is to

a. learning   **b.** accident   **c.** method   **d.** teaching

COMPLETE THE STORY

>>>> *Here are the ten vocabulary words for this lesson:*

astonished	suite	technique	individuality	components
contradictory	adhered	leeway	adjusted	immersed

>>>> *There are six blank spaces in the story below. Four vocabulary words have already been used in the story. They are underlined. Use the other six words to fill in the blanks.*

Various <u>components</u> of the evening did not go together. In fact, they seemed _____contradictory_____. The program to be played was all classical music, including a Bach _____suite_____. Those in the audience who knew Yo Yo Ma were not _____astonished_____ by his casual dress. They knew he had not <u>adhered</u> to the conventional way of doing things for a while. They knew he often expressed his <u>individuality</u> through his clothes, as well as through his music. Even the most conservative music lovers _____adjusted_____ to Ma's unusual style of dress for a concert. They were willing to give Ma some _____leeway_____. They marveled at his <u>technique</u>. As soon as he began to play, they only wanted to be _____immersed_____ in his brilliant music making.

Learn More About Artists

>>>> *On a separate sheet of paper or in your notebook or journal, complete one or more of the activities below.*

Appreciating Diversity

Yo Yo Ma had trouble adjusting to the differences between the traditional values of his family and the culture he found outside his home. What differences do you find between the values at home and those of the society at large? What are some ways you try to deal with the differences?

Learning Across the Curriculum

Why does someone become a violinist and another person an engineer? Some people believe some of these choices are made because of the way our brains work. Find out about the research of scientists who have studied people who are "left brained" or "right brained." Describe the difference. Do you think you fit one of these categories?

Extending Your Reading

Read one of these books about famous artists. Then write a short summary of his or her life. What obstacles did he or she have to overcome? What helped him or her succeed?

Scott Joplin, by Katherine Preston
Wolfgang Amadeus Mozart, by Wendy Thompson
Paul Gauguin, by Howard Greenfield
Frieda Kahlo, by Robyn Montana Turner

13 BARBRA STREISAND

Barbra Streisand is a huge success as an actress, a singer, a comedienne, and a producer. Whether she appears in a concert, a film, or a play, **ardent** fans follow her. They've been entertained by *Funny Girl, The Way We Were, A Star is Born, Nuts,* and *Prince of Tides*. All of these films display her **multiple** talents. Working until she reaches **perfection** is a Streisand **trait.** So is trying new things.

Streisand began by singing old standards. Today she is part of the **contemporary** music scene. Recently, she completed her first concert tour in 28 years. Her performance drew huge audiences and was shown on HBO.

At one point, Streisand took the biggest gamble of her career. She filmed the movie *Yentl*. In *Yentl,* a young girl poses as a man in order to study the **Talmud** in a Jewish school in Poland.

Streisand had wanted to make this film for 14 years. Many people thought it would fail, but she ignored such **prophecies.** When it comes to her career, she trusts her own **insight,** rather than the most expert adviser.

Finally, she convinced a film company to finance *Yentl*. Her work in the film was **complex.** Streisand was the star, the director, and the producer. *Yentl* was a great success. The project **revived** her spirits and helped her accomplish yet another dream.

UNDERSTANDING THE STORY

 Circle the letter next to each correct statement.

1. The statement that best expresses the main idea of this selection is:
   a. Barbra Streisand is a talented actress but a better singer.
   b. Streisand believes in her talent and ideas and will take risks in her career.
   c. If her project *Yentl* had failed, Barbra Streisand would have been finished in films.

2. From this story, you can conclude that
   a. *Yentl* was a smash hit and had a long run at the box office.
   b. Streisand will lose financial backing from film companies if she has too many failures.
   c. Streisand's talent and hard work make her a continuing favorite.

75

MAKE AN ALPHABETICAL LIST

>>>> *Here are the ten vocabulary words in this lesson. Write them in alphabetical order in the spaces below.*

ardent	contemporary	multiple	insight	perfection
complex	Talmud	trait	prophecies	revived

1. _____ardent_____
2. _____complex_____
3. _____contemporary_____
4. _____insight_____
5. _____multiple_____

6. _____perfection_____
7. _____prophecies_____
8. _____revived_____
9. _____Talmud_____
10. _____trait_____

WHAT DO THE WORDS MEAN?

>>>> *Following are some meanings, or definitions, for the ten vocabulary words in this lesson. Write the words next to their definitions.*

1. _____multiple_____ more than one; many

2. _____perfection_____ freedom from errors; excellence

3. _____insight_____ judgment; clear understanding

4. _____Talmud_____ the writings of Jewish law and history

5. _____contemporary_____ modern; of today

6. _____ardent_____ eager; filled with enthusiasm and feeling

7. _____prophecies_____ predictions; forecasts on the basis of religious inspiration

8. _____complex_____ having many parts; complicated

9. _____trait_____ a distinguishing quality; a characteristic

10. _____revived_____ renewed; refreshed

COMPLETE THE SENTENCES

>>>> *Use the vocabulary words in this lesson to complete the following sentences. Use each word only once.*

ardent	contemporary	multiple	insight	perfection
prophecies	Talmud	trait	revived	complex

1. Some movie companies made _____prophecies_____ that Streisand's motion picture *Yentl* would be a failure.

2. As a producer, Streisand must hire many people; her job is very _____complex_____.

3. Yentl dresses as a boy in the picture because, in those times, girls were not allowed to study the _____Talmud_____.

4. Barbra Streisand tries to achieve _____perfection_____ in all her work.

5. She has mastered _____contemporary_____ musical styles.

6. The support she has received has _____revived_____ her interest in making movies.

7. Very few actresses or singers have the _____multiple_____ talents of Streisand.

8. People of all generations are Streisand's _____ardent_____ fans.

9. She has always relied on her own _____insight_____ when it comes to her career.

10. Her concern for excellence is a well-known _____trait_____.

USE YOUR OWN WORDS

>>>> *Look at the picture. What words come into your mind? Write them on the lines below. To help you get started, here are two good words:*

1. _____fingernails_____
2. _____smile_____
3. _____Answers will vary._____
4. _____
5. _____
6. _____
7. _____
8. _____
9. _____
10. _____

77

MAKE POSSESSIVE WORDS

>>>> The singular possessive of a word shows that something belongs to it. For example, Bill has a boat, so it is *Bill's* boat. To make a singular word possessive, add an apostrophe and an *s* to the word, such as *baker's* bread or *class's* teacher. To make a plural word that ends in s possesive, add an apostrophe only, such as *friends'* bicycles or *ladies'* hats. To make a plural word that does not end in s possesive, add an apostrophe and an *s*, such as *children's* toys.

>>>> *Here are ten words from the story. In the space next to each word, write the correct possessive of the word.*

1. fans   fans'
2. Streisand   Streisand's
3. singers   singers'
4. company   company's
5. producers   producers'

6. actress   actress's
7. director   director's
8. plays   plays'
9. adviser   adviser's
10. career   career's

COMPLETE THE STORY

>>>> Here are the ten vocabulary words for this lesson:

ardent	perfection	complex	revived	contemporary
multiple	trait	Talmud	insight	prophecies

>>>> *There are six blank spaces in the story below. Four vocabulary words have already been used in the story. They are underlined. Use the other six words to fill in the blanks.*

Barbra Streisand, like the heroine she played in *Funny Girl,* is a woman of _____multiple_____ talents. She demands <u>perfection</u> of herself, whether she is recording a hit song or directing a movie. She has learned to rely on her own _____insight_____, rather than on the advice of others.

In her film *Yentl,* she dealt with a sensitive girl's ambition to study the ancient religious text, the _____Talmud_____. Some people in the film industry made _____prophecies_____ that this film would fail. However, Streisand, who took on the <u>complex</u> role of director, star, and producer, thought they were all wrong.

A strong _____trait_____ of Streisand's is her need to strive for excellence in all her work. Streisand has a large following of <u>ardent</u> fans of all ages. She has sung everything from Chopin to _____contemporary_____ show tunes. Her great success with *The Broadway Album* has <u>revived</u> her interest in the record business.

78

Learn More About Entertainment

>>>> *On a separate sheet of paper or in your notebook or journal, complete one or more of the activities below.*

Learning Across the Curriculum

When a big-budget movie comes out, viewers wonder how moviemakers can spend tens of millions of dollars on one movie. Check out a book from a library about the movie business, or do some reading in magazines, to find out. Then write a summary of the costs of making a movie.

Broadening Your Understanding

Research more about Barbra Streisand, Bette Midler, or some other actor/singer. List the different projects he or she has done in his or her career. Then imagine you are the agent of this person. Write a letter advising what the actor/singer should do next and why.

Extending Your Reading

Read one of the following plays or read another one. Would this play make a good movie? Explain why. Then describe how you would change the play to make it a better movie.

When the Rattlesnake Sounds, by Alice Childress
Escape to Freedom, by Ossie Davis
East of the Sun and West of the Moon, by Nancy Williard
Holiday in the Rain Forest and Kabuki Gift, by Douglas Love

14 SOCCER

Do you play soccer? If so, you have a lot of *potential* teammates. In 1993, even before the World Cup came to the United States, 16,400 Americans played soccer. For young Americans, soccer is now the fourth most popular sport, after basketball, volleyball, and softball, and ahead of baseball. To *confirm* this growing passion, *registration* for soccer leagues has risen by 170 percent since 1980.

Although soccer players are mostly in other nations, two of every five U.S. players are female. In fact, the *superb* U.S. women's team is the reigning world champion, beating China for the women's title in 1991.

In the summer of 1994, the World Cup tournament was held in the United States for the first time ever. Twenty-four teams, each representing a different nation, were chosen to compete for the World Cup championship, which is usually held every four years. The series of 52 games caused a *frenzy* of interest in soccer in this country.

By the time the World Cup was over, U.S. fans were *elated* by their team's *impressive* success. In the first round of play, the U.S. team tied Switzerland, beat a highly rated Colombian team, and lost to Romania. In the second round of play, the U.S. team lost to Brazil, the team that went on to win the World Cup.

The *multitude* of soccer fans in this country are hoping the excitement of the World Cup will be an *incentive* to establish major league soccer in North America. Even without a major league, however, the *verdict* is in: Soccer is here to stay!

UNDERSTANDING THE STORY

>>>> *Circle the letter next to each correct statement.*

1. The statement that best expresses the main idea of this selection is:
   a. Soccer was not popular in the United States before the World Cup was held here.
   b. The World Cup helped increase interest in soccer in the United States.
   c. Soccer has always been a popular sport for girls and women.

2. From this story, you can conclude that
   a. an increasing number of schools are adding soccer to their sports programs.
   b. many fans lost interest in soccer when the U.S. team did not win the World Cup.
   c. a major league for soccer would spoil the sport for amateurs.

MAKE AN ALPHABETICAL LIST

>>>> *Here are the ten vocabulary words in this lesson. Write them in alphabetical order in the spaces below.*

verdict	multitude	registration	potential	incentive
confirm	elated	frenzy	impressive	superb

1. confirm
2. elated
3. frenzy
4. impressive
5. incentive
6. multitude
7. potential
8. registration
9. superb
10. verdict

WHAT DO THE WORDS MEAN?

>>>> *Following are some meanings, or definitions, for the ten vocabulary words in this lesson. Write the words next to their definitions.*

1. incentive — a reason for doing something
2. elated — excited; joyful
3. superb — excellent
4. confirm — to approve; to remove doubt
5. verdict — a judgment or an opinion
6. registration — enrollment; signing up
7. impressive — admirable; deserving credit
8. potential — possible
9. multitude — a great number
10. frenzy — temporary madness; wild activity

82

COMPLETE THE SENTENCES

>>>> *Use the vocabulary words in this lesson to complete the following sentences. Use each word only once.*

registration	verdict	confirm	incentive	multitude
potential	elated	impressive	frenzy	superb

1. The World Cup has interested a _____multitude_____ of people in soccer.

2. One _____potential_____ outcome of the World Cup may be a major soccer league in the United States.

3. Income from commercials during televised soccer games may be an _____incentive_____ for large companies to help finance teams.

4. The organizers of the World Cup were caught in a _____frenzy_____.

5. The World Cup sponsors are _____elated_____ about the number of people who attended the games.

6. High attendance at the games has helped to _____confirm_____ the high interest in the sport.

7. Although the U.S. soccer team did not win the World Cup, its performance was _____impressive_____.

8. The _____verdict_____ on the World Cup games is that they were successful.

9. _____Registration_____ in national soccer leagues should continue to increase.

10. The U.S. women's championship team is rated as _____superb_____ worldwide.

USE YOUR OWN WORDS

>>>> *Look at the picture. What words come into your mind? Write them on the lines below. To help you get started, here are two good words:*

1. _____competitive_____
2. _____skilled_____
3. _____Answers will vary._____
4. _____
5. _____
6. _____
7. _____
8. _____
9. _____
10. _____

FIND THE ADJECTIVES

>>>> An **adjective** is a word that describes a person, place, or thing. The adjectives in the following sentences are underlined: The <u>thrilled</u> fans cheered (person). The game was held in a <u>huge</u> stadium (place). The <u>increasing</u> interest may lead to a <u>major</u> league (things).

>>>> *Underline the adjectives in the following sentences.*

1. The <u>elated</u> fans cheered for their <u>battling</u> team.

2. In <u>other</u> nations, <u>most</u> <u>soccer</u> players are men.

3. <u>Skilled</u> teams from <u>24</u> nations played in the games.

4. The <u>courageous</u> <u>American</u> team put on an <u>impressive</u> performance.

5. Soccer is becoming a <u>popular</u> sport among <u>young</u> and <u>not-so-young</u> Americans.

COMPLETE THE STORY

>>>> Here are the ten vocabulary words for this lesson:

confirm	superb	registration	frenzy	impressive
multitude	verdict	elated	incentive	potential

>>>> *There are six blank spaces in the story below. Four vocabulary words have already been used in the story. They are underlined. Use the other six words to fill in the blanks.*

Across the nation, the increasing __registration__ in soccer leagues seems to __confirm__ the high interest in this sport. So many young people are playing that soon the United States will have a <u>superb</u> team with the __potential__ to win the World Cup. The girls' and women's teams are also <u>impressive</u> and soon may want a major league of their own. Members of the U.S. women's team were __elated__ when they won the first worldwide women's soccer championship.

The __multitude__ of fans who went into a <u>frenzy</u> over the World Cup games might agree on one <u>verdict</u>: Soccer is exciting. The thrill they got from those games gives them an __incentive__ to keep watching.

84

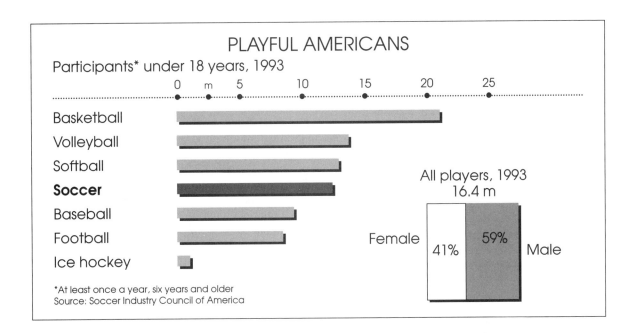

PLAYFUL AMERICANS

Participants* under 18 years, 1993

Basketball
Volleyball
Softball
Soccer
Baseball
Football
Ice hockey

All players, 1993
16.4 m

Female 41% 59% Male

*At least once a year, six years and older
Source: Soccer Industry Council of America

Learn More About Soccer

>>>> *On a separate sheet of paper or in your notebook or journal, complete one or more of the activities below.*

Learning Across the Curriculum

Use the bar graph and pie chart to answer these questions:
1. Which sport is about as popular with young people as soccer is? _____ softball _____
2. Which sport has nearly 10 million young players? _____ baseball _____
3. In 1993, what percent of soccer players was female? _____ 41 per cent _____

Broadening Your Understanding

Find out more about the background and training of a successful male or female soccer player. Research a current or former player from the United States or another nation. Share what you learn with the class. Then discuss the similarities discovered among players of both genders and all nationalities.

Extending Your Reading

Soccer Around the World, by Dale E. Howard
This book traces the success of soccer teams from the United States and eight other countries. After reading it, compare the history of U.S. teams with the history of teams from another country.

Soccer: From Neighborhood Play to the World Cup, by Caroline Arnold
This author focuses on soccer in the United States and describes basic soccer skills and different soccer leagues. After reading the book, find out how many of the opportunities to play soccer described in the book are available in your community.

15 ATHENS' GLORY

Modern Athens is a city of great **contrasts.** It has new buildings and wide roads. But Athens also retains the beauty of its ancient past when Greece was a powerful center of civilization.

Rising high above the city is the Acropolis, a hill that towers 200 feet above the rest of Athens. The Acropolis has some of the most beautiful and **imposing** buildings in the world. One of them is the Parthenon, a temple built about 2,500 years ago to honor the goddess Athena, **guardian** of the ancient city.

The **exterior** of the temple was made of marble with tall Doric columns on each side. At the center of the Parthenon stood a great gold and ivory statue of Athena. The inner walls of the structure were decorated with a carved scene of a festival in honor of this goddess.

The Parthenon was filled with **ornate** works of art. Red, blue, and gold pieces of **sculpture** glorified the Greek gods.

The Parthenon was well preserved for many centuries. But in 1687, Athens was attacked, and part of this great building was **demolished.** Many of its sculptures were later taken to London.

But the **heritage** of Greece still lives on in the Parthenon. Visitors from all over the world travel to Athens each year to see this building. They **wend** their way through souvenir peddlers and climb to the top of the Acropolis. Standing there, partly worn with age, partly destroyed by war, but still noble and proud, is the **exalted** Parthenon.

UNDERSTANDING THE STORY

>>>> *Circle the letter next to each correct statement.*

1. The statement that best expresses the main idea of this selection is:
   a. The ivory and gold statue of Athena is the glory of the Parthenon.
   b. The destruction of the Parthenon and many of its sculptures has reduced their historical value.
   c. Despite the damage, the Parthenon still remains a beautiful structure of which the Greeks are very proud.

2. From this story, you can conclude that
   a. the Parthenon, in its original condition, must have been one of the most beautiful buildings in ancient Greece.
   b. the Greek government will try to restore the Parthenon to its original condition.
   c. buildings like the Parthenon can be seen all over Greece.

MAKE AN ALPHABETICAL LIST

>>>> *Here are the ten vocabulary words in this lesson. Write them in alphabetical order in the spaces below.*

sculpture imposing wend exterior contrasts	
ornate guardian heritage demolished exalted	

1. _____contrasts_____
2. _____demolished_____
3. _____exalted_____
4. _____exterior_____
5. _____guardian_____

6. _____heritage_____
7. _____imposing_____
8. _____ornate_____
9. _____sculpture_____
10. _____wend_____

WHAT DO THE WORDS MEAN?

>>>> *Following are some meanings, or definitions, for the ten vocabulary words in this lesson. Write the words next to their definitions.*

1. _____heritage_____ something passed from one generation to the next
2. _____exterior_____ outside
3. _____imposing_____ impressive because of size or greatness
4. _____exalted_____ noble; grand and important
5. _____contrasts_____ great differences
6. _____ornate_____ having much detail; elaborate
7. _____demolished_____ destroyed; torn down
8. _____guardian_____ one who watches, protects, and takes care of
9. _____wend_____ to travel; to move along a route
10. _____sculpture_____ carved or molded artwork

COMPLETE THE SENTENCES

>>>> *Use the vocabulary words in this lesson to complete the following sentences. Use each word only once.*

contrasts	sculpture	imposing	demolished	guardian
wend	exterior	exalted	ornate	heritage

1. The _____contrasts_____ between the original Parthenon and the ruins of today are enormous.

2. With the large gold statue of Athena in it, the Parthenon must have been even more _____imposing_____ than it is today.

3. As the _____guardian_____ of the city, Athena protected Athens.

4. The _____exterior_____ of this beautiful structure was made of marble.

5. During a war, an attack on Athens _____demolished_____ a good part of this temple.

6. The most famous building in Greece is the _____exalted_____ Parthenon.

7. The Parthenon and its sculptures are part of Greece's ancient _____heritage_____.

8. The interior of this temple contained many _____ornate_____ works of art.

9. It is interesting to watch tourists _____wend_____ their way to the top of the hill.

10. The artists of ancient Greece illustrated legends of their country in the many pieces of _____sculpture_____ created for the Parthenon.

USE YOUR OWN WORDS

>>>> *Look at the picture. What words come into your mind? Write them on the lines below. To help you get started, here are two good words:*

1. _____chimneys_____
2. _____construction_____
3. _____Answers will vary._____
4. _____
5. _____
6. _____
7. _____
8. _____
9. _____
10. _____

DO THE CROSSWORD PUZZLE

>>>> *In a crossword puzzle, there is a group of boxes, some with numbers in them. There are also two columns of words or definitions, one for "Across" and the other for "Down." Do the puzzle. Each of the words in the puzzle will be one of the 10 vocabulary words in this lesson.*

Across

1. carved artwork

3. elaborate

5. something passed through generations

6. travel

Down

2. great differences

4. noble; grand

```
  1 s 2 c  u  l  p  t  u  r  e
        o
  3 o  r  n  a  t 4 e
        t           x
  5 h  e  r  i  t  a  g  e
        a           l
        s           t
        t     6 w  e  n  d
        s           d
```

COMPLETE THE STORY

>>>> Here are the ten vocabulary words for this lesson:

contrast	exalted	heritage	ornate	imposing
sculpture	wend	guardian	demolished	exterior

>>>> *There are six blank spaces in the story below. Four vocabulary words have already been used in the story. They are underlined. Use the other six words to fill in the blanks.*

Imagine the beauty of ancient Greece! The Parthenon is just one of many _____imposing_____ sights. Although part of the temple was demolished, much of the _____ornate_____ artwork remains. The building's marble exterior shows us that the ancient Greeks were skilled craftsworkers. The _____sculpture_____ of Athena indicated that they were also a religious people. The Parthenon was a temple, built to honor the goddess Athena, the _____guardian_____ of the city.

The Parthenon shows that Athens is a city of exciting contrasts. Not only are there ancient buildings that belong to the _____heritage_____ of the city, but there are many modern structures as well. In a single day, tourists can see buildings from both the past and the present. They can visit libraries and museums in modern Athens. Then they can wend their way to the top of the Acropolis. There they can visit one of the most _____exalted_____ of all buildings, the magnificent Parthenon.

Learn More About Greece

>>>> *On a separate sheet of paper or in your notebook or journal, complete one or more of the activities below.*

Learning Across the Curriculum

Find out more about the world in which the Parthenon was built. Research the life of people in Greece 2,500 years ago and write how it differs from yours.

Broadening Your Understanding

Imagine you will be the tour guide on a trip through modern Athens. Research more about this city and write what kind of historic sites you will show tourists and why.

Further Reading

Read one of these books about ancient Greek mythology. Then retell your favorite myth in your own words.

The Macmillan Book of Greek Gods and Heroes, by Alice Low
Tales the Muses Told, by Roger Green
Greek Myths, by Ellen Switzer

16 HEALER OF MANY

The year was 1921. Franklin Roosevelt rested in bed, *stricken* with a disease that attacked thousands of people each year. For months, his legs were *paralyzed.* Years later, as President of the United States, Roosevelt had to be pushed in a wheelchair. At that time, there was no way to prevent this crippling disease—polio.

In 1951, a bright young doctor, Jonas Salk, began to work on a polio *vaccine.* He knew there must be a way to make people *immune* to polio. Dr. Salk wanted to develop a vaccine that would kill all three kinds of the polio *virus.*

Dr. Salk worked *diligently* for two years. Finally, he found a vaccine that he thought would prevent *infection.* Salk, his wife, and their three sons were the first to test it. The results were promising. The vaccine appeared to be safe.

Almost 2 million school children took part in further testing. This program was *sponsored* by the National Foundation for Infantile Paralysis, a group that President Roosevelt had helped to start. In April 1955, after studying all the test results, a team of doctors *asserted* that the vaccine was both safe and effective. Polio could now be prevented.

Dr. Salk received honors from all over the world. He was even given a special *citation* from President Dwight Eisenhower. But Dr. Salk did not stop there. Recently, he tested a vaccine for AIDS. If this new vaccine works, Dr. Salk will have helped save thousands more lives.

UNDERSTANDING THE STORY

>>>> *Circle the letter next to each correct statement.*

1. The statement that best expresses the main idea of this selection is:
   a. Dr. Salk's diligent research resulted in preventing polio.
   b. The National Foundation for Infantile Paralysis sponsored Salk's research.
   c. Before the development of the Salk vaccine, thousands of people were crippled by the disease.

2. From this story, you can conclude that
   a. Dr. Salk is devoted to helping humanity through his research.
   b. Dr. Salk is certain to make other scientific discoveries.
   c. infantile paralysis may break out again as other diseases have in the past.

MAKE AN ALPHABETICAL LIST

>>>> *Here are the ten vocabulary words in this lesson. Write them in alphabetical order in the spaces below.*

vaccine	asserted	paralyzed	infection	virus
immune	stricken	citation	sponsored	diligently

1. asserted
2. citation
3. diligently
4. immune
5. infection

6. paralyzed
7. sponsored
8. stricken
9. vaccine
10. virus

WHAT DO THE WORDS MEAN?

>>>> *Following are some meanings, or definitions, for the ten vocabulary words in this lesson. Write the words next to their definitions.*

1. virus _____ something within body cells that causes disease
2. sponsored _____ supported; helped
3. vaccine _____ a medical preparation that prevents disease
4. citation _____ a formal statement that honors a person
5. infection _____ the process of causing disease
6. asserted _____ stated positively; said with confidence
7. stricken _____ hit or hurt, usually by a disease or misfortune
8. paralyzed _____ unable to move; made powerless
9. diligently _____ carefully, steadily, and earnestly
10. immune _____ protected from something, usually a disease

94

COMPLETE THE SENTENCES

>>>> *Use the vocabulary words in this lesson to complete the following sentences. Use each word only once.*

stricken	diligently	paralyzed	infection	immune
sponsored	vaccine	asserted	virus	citation

1. Unless the patient was given immediate care, the ____infection____ would spread.
2. One of the most dreadful results of having polio was being ____paralyzed____.
3. Before Salk's vaccine, no one was ____immune____ to polio.
4. The Salk ____vaccine____ is one of the great medical achievements of this century.
5. If polio research had not been ____sponsored____, the cure might have been delayed a long time.
6. The doctors who studied the Salk vaccine ____asserted____ that it was safe to use.
7. For many years, Dr. Salk worked ____diligently____ on preventing polio.
8. Franklin Roosevelt was ____stricken____ with polio at the age of 39.
9. President Dwight D. Eisenhower gave a special ____citation____ to Dr. Salk for his tremendous achievement.
10. Everyone is grateful to Dr. Salk for finding out how to kill the polio ____virus____.

USE YOUR OWN WORDS

>>>> *Look at the picture. What words come into your mind other than the ten vocabulary words used in this lesson? Write them on the lines below. To help you get started, here are two good words:*

1. ____tie____
2. ____smock____
3. ____Answers will vary.____
4. _____
5. _____
6. _____
7. _____
8. _____
9. _____
10. _____

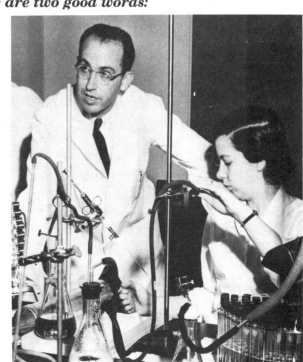

MAKE NEW WORDS FROM OLD

>>>> *Look at the vocabulary word below. See how many words you can form by using the letters of this word. Make up at least ten words. Write your words in the spaces below.*

diligently

1. _____line_____
2. _____dent_____
3. _____gently_____
4. _____lent_____
5. _____glen_____
6. _____lily_____

7. _____end_____
8. _____lend_____
9. _____yell_____
10. _____glide_____
11. _____lie_____
12. _____leg_____

COMPLETE THE STORY

>>>> Here are the ten vocabulary words for this lesson:

sponsored	asserted	virus	vaccine	infection
paralyzed	immune	citation	diligently	stricken

>>>> *There are six blank spaces in the story below. Four vocabulary words have already been used in the story. They are underlined. Use the other six words to fill in the blanks.*

Dr. Jonas Salk brought relief to millions when he developed a ____vaccine____ to prevent polio. He searched ____diligently____ for a solution that would make people immune to this crippling disease. Dr. Salk succeeded when he found a way to kill the polio ____virus____. He was never really alone in his search. His work was ____sponsored____ by the National Foundation for Infantile Paralysis, which gave him $1,700,000 to help his research.

When it was asserted that the polio vaccine was effective in preventing infection, Dr. Salk was given a special ____citation____. Thanks to Dr. Salk, people are no longer afraid that they will be paralyzed by this disease. Thanks to this dedicated doctor, thousands are no longer ____paralyzed____ by polio.

96

Learn More About Diseases

>>>> *On a separate sheet of paper or in your notebook or journal, complete one or more of the activities below.*

Learning Across the Curriculum

What is a vaccine? How does it work? Find out the science behind vaccines and explain it in a paragraph.

Broadening Your Understanding

As a child, you were immunized against several diseases. Find out what diseases children are immunized against today and why. Ask your school nurse or doctor for more information.

Extending Your Reading

Read one of these books about Dr. Salk's polio vaccine and how he developed it. Then write a one-act play about Dr. Salk's invention of the vaccine.

Jonas Salk, by Marjorie Curson
Jonas Salk: Discoverer of the Polio Vaccine, by Carmen Bredeson
The Story of Jonas Salk, by Jim Hargrove

17 MARGARET MEAD

Dr. Margaret Mead was an anthropologist who studied the customs and cultures of people all over the world. At the age of 23, Mead first sailed for Samoa in the South Seas. She especially wanted to learn about the adolescents, or teenagers, in this part of the world. For nine months, Mead lived among the Samoan people. They helped her build a house without walls so that she could observe their daily lives. Dr. Mead watched the way they reared their children. She listened and took notes without imposing her own views. The Samoans trusted her and respected her work.

During her long career, Dr. Mead studied seven tribes in the South Seas. She compared their differences and similarities. In her conclusions, Dr. Mead noted that these people lived happy lives. Their children seemed free from torment. They did not have the conflicts and problems of many American teenagers.

Margaret Mead wrote books based on her studies. Some became best-sellers, such as *Coming of Age in Samoa, From the South Seas,* and *Growing Up in New Guinea.*

In the 1920s, Dr. Mead was the first woman working in a scientific field dominated by men, but that didn't hinder her. Instead, she became the leading authority in her field.

When Dr. Mead died, people all over the world mourned her. As far away as Manus Island in the Pacific, drums beat out a death song for this beloved and honored woman.

UNDERSTANDING THE STORY

>>>> *Circle the letter next to each correct statement.*

1. The statement that best expresses the main idea of this selection is:
   a. The lives of Samoans are no different from the lives of Americans.
   b. Dr. Mead succeeded in the field of anthropology because she was the first to visit the South Seas.
   c. Dr. Mead's skills as an anthropologist helped her to study the cultures of the South Seas.

2. From this story, you can conclude that
   a. Dr. Mead's studies will continue to be important to other anthropologists.
   b. more students will become anthropologists because they want to visit other countries.
   c. the people of the South Seas will not welcome any more studies of their customs.

MAKE AN ALPHABETICAL LIST

>>>> *Here are the ten vocabulary words in this lesson. Write them in alphabetical order in the spaces below.*

adolescents	similarities	anthropologist	mourned	conclusion
conflicts	hinder	imposing	reared	torment

1. adolescents
2. anthropologist
3. conclusions
4. conflicts
5. hinder

6. imposing
7. mourned
8. reared
9. similarities
10. torment

WHAT DO THE WORDS MEAN?

>>>> *Following are some meanings, or definitions, for the ten vocabulary words in this lesson. Write the words next to their definitions.*

1. adolescents — teenagers; young people between the ages of 12 and 17

2. anthropologist — one who studies the customs and cultures of different peoples

3. mourned — grieved; felt sad over someone's death

4. conflicts — struggles; strong disagreements

5. torment — suffering; great pain

6. hinder — to get in the way; block

7. reared — raised; brought up

8. imposing — forcing one's opinions or actions upon another

9. similarities — likenesses; things that are almost the same

10. conclusions — reasoned judgments; opinions based on facts

>>>> *Use the vocabulary words in this lesson to complete the following sentences. Use each word only once.*

anthropologist	similarities	conclusions	conflicts	hinder
mourned	torment	reared	imposing	adolescents

1. When Margaret Mead died, people from many lands _____mourned_____ her passing.
2. The people of the South Seas _____reared_____ their children differently.
3. Dr. Mead's study of a culture different from her own did not
   _____hinder_____ her.
4. Dr. Mead found that _____adolescents_____ growing up in the South Seas islands were happy.
5. The _____conclusions_____ that Dr. Mead reached were published in *Coming of Age in Somoa*.
6. An _____anthropologist_____ studies human nature, culture, and customs.
7. Dr. Mead found differences and _____similarities_____ among the tribes.
8. When anthropologists study a foreign culture, they must do so without
   _____imposing_____ their own ideas and opinions.
9. Dr. Mead found that there were few _____conflicts_____ among families on the islands.
10. A Samoan teenager felt _____torment_____ at the thought of leaving the island.

USE YOUR OWN WORDS

>>>> *Look at the picture. What words come into your mind? Write them on the lines below. To help you get started, here are two good words:*

1. _____corsage_____
2. _____watch_____
3. ___Answers will vary.___
4. _____
5. _____
6. _____
7. _____
8. _____
9. _____
10. _____

DO THE CROSSWORD PUZZLE

>>>> *In a crossword puzzle, there is a group of boxes, some with numbers in them. There are also two columns of words or definitions, one for "Across" and the other for "Down." Do the puzzle. Each of the words in the puzzle will be one of the vocabulary words in this lesson.*

Across

1. some teenagers
3. get in the way
6. suffering
7. forcing one's will upon another

Down

2. strong disagreements
4. raised
5. judgments

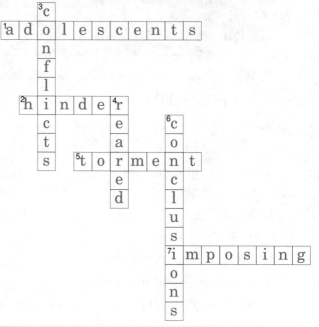

COMPLETE THE STORY

>>>> Here are the ten vocabulary words for this lesson:

conflicts	imposing	anthropologist	similarities	adolescents
hinder	torment	reared	conclusions	mourned

>>>> *There are six blank spaces in the story below. Four vocabulary words have already been used in the story. They are underlined. Use the other six words to fill in the blanks.*

An _____anthropologist_____ studies the customs and behavior of people in different cultures. When Dr. Margaret Mead entered the field, it was dominated by men. But this did not <u>hinder</u> her. She wanted to study the _____adolescents_____ of Samoa. She was impressed by the way the Samoans <u>reared</u> their children. There were few _____conflicts_____ between children or among families. <u>Torment</u> only occurred when families had to be separated.

Without <u>imposing</u> her own ideas, Dr. Mead got a realistic picture of life in the South Seas. When she returned to the United States, she published _____conclusions_____ based on her studies. Her books compared the differences and _____similarities_____ among cultures in the South Seas. When Dr. Mead died in 1978, people from many lands _____mourned_____ her.

Learn More About Anthropology

>>>> *On a separate sheet of paper or in your notebook or journal, complete one or more of the activities below.*

Learning Across the Curriculum

Carbon-dating is a method anthropologists use to learn the age of something. Write a description of how carbon-14-dating works and how it has been useful for anthropologists.

Broadening Your Understanding

Learn more about the life of Margaret Mead. Why did she become an anthropologist? What helped her succeed in her field? How could you use some of the lessons of her life to help you succeed in a career?

Extending Your Reading

English anthropologist Jane Goodall has spent her life studying wild chimpanzees and their social behavior. Read one of her books or a book about her work. Write a summary of what she has learned about the similarity of these animals' behavior to human behavior.

My Life with the Chimpanzees, by Jane Goodall
The Chimpanzee Family Book, by Jane Goodall
Walking with the Great Apes: Jane Goodall, by Sy Montgomery
Wild Animals, Gentle Woman, by Margery Facklam

He was one of the most ambitious artists ever to place paint on a canvas. He painted in so many *varied* styles that it is hard to believe all his paintings were done by one man. He painted *morbid* clowns and strange-looking musicians. He studied primitive African sculpture and colorful pottery. With a friend, he started a new style of painting called *cubism.* His name was Pablo Picasso.

Picasso was born in Spain. He started art school when he was 15. His first teacher was his father, who was a professor at the school. As a young man, Picasso moved to Paris, where he attracted a great deal of attention because of the *vitality* of his art. He remained in that city throughout World War II. After the war, he became interested in *ceramics* and began to make different kinds of pottery.

Picasso's early work in cubism was different from anything else that had ever been done before. These paintings used only *geometric* shapes, such as cubes and cones. Reality was not important to Picasso. The idea of his art was to create images from just a few basic shapes.

One of Picasso's most famous paintings is his *Guernica*. It is a scene that *depicts* the horror of the Spanish Civil War of 1936. This painting, like most of Picasso's other works, has *universal* appeal. It is an *intriguing* study of war that can be understood by all people.

An ambitious and *inventive* man, Picasso changed the world of art. He produced more than 600 paintings before his death at the age of 91. They will surely live on, for he was a universal artist.

UNDERSTANDING THE STORY

>>>> *Circle the letter next to each correct statement.*

1. The statement that best expresses the main idea of this selection is:
   a. Picasso invented cubism, a new style of painting that influenced many painters.
   b. *Guernica* is one of the greatest paintings about war.
   c. Pablo Picasso was a painter whose many styles greatly influenced modern art.

2. From this story, you can conclude that
   a. museums throughout the world will continue to feature Picasso's paintings in their exhibits.
   b. cubism is a painting style that will become popular again.
   c. if Picasso had lived even longer, he would have spent most of his time on sculpture instead of painting.

MAKE AN ALPHABETICAL LIST

>>>> *Here are the ten vocabulary words in this lesson. Write them in alphabetical order in the spaces below.*

geometric	inventive	morbid	depicts	ceramics
universal	cubism	varied	vitality	intriguing

1. ceramics
2. cubism
3. depicts
4. geometric
5. intriguing

6. inventive
7. morbid
8. universal
9. varied
10. vitality

WHAT DO THE WORDS MEAN?

>>>> *Following are some meanings, or definitions, for the ten vocabulary words in this lesson. Write the words next to their definitions.*

1. cubism — a type of painting that uses only lines and simple shapes

2. universal — worldwide; belonging to or having to do with all people

3. intriguing — very interesting; fascinating

4. ceramics — the art of making pottery, usually from clay

5. depicts — shows; represents

6. varied — different; of many types

7. vitality — energy; liveliness

8. geometric — made from or related to simple shapes

9. morbid — very gloomy

10. inventive — creative; able to make new things

COMPLETE THE SENTENCES

>>>> *Use the vocabulary words in this lesson to complete the following sentences. Use each word only once.*

varied	ceramics	morbid	depicts	cubism
intriguing	vitality	inventive	geometric	universal

1. At times, Pablo Picasso liked to paint _____morbid_____ pictures of clowns.

2. _____Ceramics_____ is the art of making pottery.

3. Picasso had tremendous _____vitality_____, that enabled him to work in many styles.

4. *Guernica* is a masterpiece that _____depicts_____ the horrors of war.

5. Picasso's clowns are _____geometric_____ portraits of circus performers.

6. His many _____inventive_____ styles reveal that Picasso believed in change and experimentation.

7. _____Cubism_____ distorts the shapes and sizes of objects to form striking images.

8. Cubes, cones, and triangles are some of the _____varied_____ forms and shapes used by cubists.

9. His paintings have a _____universal_____ appeal to people all over the world.

10. Picasso's paintings of strange-looking musicians are very _____intriguing_____.

USE YOUR OWN WORDS

>>>> *Look at the picture. What words come into your mind? Write them on the lines below. To help you get started, here are two good words:*

1. _____watch_____
2. _____work_____
3. _____Answers will vary._____
4. _____
5. _____
6. _____
7. _____
8. _____
9. _____
10. _____

FIND THE SYNONYMS

>>>> *The story you read has many interesting words that were not underlined as vocabulary words. Can you think of a synonym for each of these words below?*

>>>> A **synonym** is a word that means the same, or nearly the same, as another word. *Sorrowful* and *sad* are synonyms. Write a synonym in the blank space next to the word.

1. shapes _Answers will vary._

2. style _____

3. contain _____

4. master _____

5. started _____

6. create _____

COMPLETE THE STORY

>>>> Here are the ten vocabulary words for this lesson:

cubism	vitality	depicts	inventive	geometric
universal	varied	morbid	intriguing	ceramics

>>>> *There are six blank spaces in the story below. Four vocabulary words have already been used in the story. They are underlined. Use the other six words to fill in the blanks.*

One sign of a truly <u>inventive</u> painter is that he or she is a master of many different styles. Pablo Picasso not only used many _____varied_____ styles of painting but also produced many different types of art. Besides painting, he made pottery and other kinds of _____ceramics_____.

Whether he worked in clay or with paint, Picasso produced art with _____universal_____ appeal. His *Guernica,* for example, _____depicts_____ a scene that people everywhere can understand. It is an _____intriguing_____ study that shows the <u>morbid</u> side of war.

Picasso will perhaps be remembered best as the man who started _____cubism_____, the art form that is based on <u>geometric</u> shapes. By finding a new way to communicate on canvas, Picasso changed the world of art. Both his life and his work were filled with a <u>vitality</u> that will long be remembered by people everywhere.

Learn More About Art

>>>> *On a separate sheet of paper or in your notebook or journal, complete one or more of the activities below.*

Building Language

Find a picture of one of Pablo Picasso's paintings. Two famous ones are *Les Demoiselles d'Avignon* and *The Three Musicians.* Describe how the painting makes you feel and tell whether you like it. Write in your native language. Then translate what you wrote into English. Do the words in English translate into what you mean? If not, use a dictionary or thesaurus to look for other words that better describe your opinions.

Learning Across the Curriculum

The Spanish Civil War of 1936 inspired what may be Pablo Picasso's most famous painting—*Guernica.* Find out more about the Spanish Civil War. Then look at a copy of Picasso's painting. What do you think he thought of this war? How does this painting relate to the Spanish Civil War and to war in general?

Broadening Your Understanding

Pablo Picasso is known for cubism, but there are a variety of other styles of European and American painting, including impressionism, realism, surrealism, and abstract expressionism. Find out more about one of these styles. Prepare an oral report for the class that includes paintings to explain the points you plan to make about the art style you are presenting.

19 A SPECIAL TEACHER

Marva Collins is an unusual teacher. She has devoted her life to helping students who have been **labeled** **unteachable.** In 1975, she started a school called Westside Prep in Chicago. Her goal was to take students who were failures in public school and make them **achievers.** Since then, she has opened three similar schools, two more in Chicago and one in Cincinnati, Ohio. The students at all these schools **recite** a **creed** every morning. At Wayside Prep, they say, "I will ignore the tags and names given me by society because only I know what I have the ability to become."

Collins believes that all her students have the ability to be **successful.** She accepts students who have had failing grades and those who have severe learning problems.

Collins believes in teaching the basic skills. Everybody at her schools must learn to read, and once they can read, they read the best books. These include the writings of Shakespeare and Chaucer and other fine works of **literature.** Collins has become famous for being able to teach **impoverished** students to read such works.

The rock star formerly known as Prince has donated money to keep her work alive. Television star Mr. T has paid **tuition** for students from the Cabrini-Green public housing project in Chicago to attend Westside Prep. Collins tries to make sure her students do the work they are supposed to do. She also believes in making them feel good about themselves. She thinks that this **combination** can make a good student out of anyone.

UNDERSTANDING THE STORY

>>>> *Circle the letter next to each correct statement.*

1. The statement that best expresses the main idea of this selection is:
   a. Marva Collins runs schools that make achievers out of failures.
   b. Marva Collins has become famous and has appeared on television.
   c. The students at Marva Collins's schools read Shakespeare and Chaucer.

2. From this story, you can conclude that
   a. students at Marva Collins's schools do not have to work very hard.
   b. Mr. T attended Westside Prep.
   c. Marva Collins cares a lot about her students' futures.

MAKE AN ALPHABETICAL LIST

>>>> *Here are the ten vocabulary words in this lesson. Write them in alphabetical order in the spaces below.*

recite	combination	unteachable	achievers	labeled
successful	creed	tuition	literature	impoverished

1. achievers
2. combination
3. creed
4. impoverished
5. labeled

6. literature
7. recite
8. successful
9. tuition
10. unteachable

WHAT DO THE WORDS MEAN?

>>>> *Following are some meanings, or definitions, for the ten vocabulary words in this lesson. Write the words next to their definitions.*

1. combination — mixture
2. impoverished — poor
3. achievers — people who accomplish something
4. literature — written works of art
5. unteachable — not able to be taught
6. recite — to say from memory
7. labeled — described as
8. tuition — money paid to go to a school
9. creed — a statement of belief
10. successful — having achieved something attempted

COMPLETE THE SENTENCES

>>>> *Use the vocabulary words in this lesson to complete the following sentences. Use each word only once.*

labeled	successful	unteachable	literature	achievers
impoverished	recite	tuition	creed	combination

1. Marva Collins tries to make _____ achievers _____ out of all her students.

2. Some of her students were considered _____ unteachable _____ in school.

3. Collins does not think students should be _____ labeled _____ failures.

4. Some students get help in paying their _____ tuition _____.

5. Collins wants students to be able to attend Westside Prep even if they come from _____ impoverished _____ families.

6. The students say the school _____ creed _____ every morning.

7. Collins believes the students should _____ recite _____ the words, "I will ignore the tags and names given me by society…" every day.

8. The students at Westside Prep learn to read fine _____ literature _____.

9. Collins uses a _____ combination _____ of good teaching and hard work.

10. Collins believes every student can be a _____ successful _____ student.

USE YOUR OWN WORDS

>>>> *Look at the picture. What words come into your mind? Write them on the lines below. To help you get started, here are two good words:*

1. _____ students _____
2. _____ teacher _____
3. _____ Answers will vary. _____
4. _____
5. _____
6. _____
7. _____
8. _____
9. _____
10. _____

>>>> *There are six vocabulary words listed below. To the right of each is either a synonym or an antonym. A **synonym** is a word that means the same, or nearly the same, as another word. An **antonym** is a word that means the opposite of another word.*

>>>> *On the line beside each pair of words, write **S** for synonyms or **A** for antonyms.*

1. **recite**	say	1.	S
2. **achievers**	failures	2.	A
3. **tuition**	cost	3.	S
4. **creed**	belief	4.	S
5. **impoverished**	rich	5.	A
6. **successful**	unsuccessful	6.	A

COMPLETE THE STORY

>>>> Here are the ten vocabulary words for this lesson:

literature	impoverished	recite	achievers	successful
creed	combination	labeled	unteachable	tuition

>>>> *There are six blank spaces in the story below. Four vocabulary words have already been used in the story. They are underlined. Use the other six words to fill in the blanks.*

Perhaps Westside Prep's most famous student was Kevin Ross. He was a very underline{successful} basketball player at Creighton University. He went to Westside Prep at the age of 23. He was one of the great _____achievers_____ on the basketball court, but as a student, he was <u>impoverished</u>. After completing four years of college, Ross not only couldn't read fine _____literature_____, he could not read at all. Ross had been _____labeled_____ a success by society, but he must have seen himself as an <u>unteachable</u> student. He probably had no trouble paying the school _____tuition_____, but he had to doubt his ability to learn.

Marva Collins believed he could learn. She had Ross _____recite_____ the <u>creed</u> every day so that he would believe in himself. This _____combination_____ of ego boosting and teaching the basics helped Ross to become an educated person.

Learn More About Teaching

>>>> *On a separate sheet of paper or in your notebook or journal, complete one or more of the activities below.*

Building Language

What do you think is the best way to teach a student in the United States whose first language is not English? Think about the way you were taught and whether you could improve it. Design a program for a student your age who is just entering the school system.

Broadening Your Understanding

Choose a skill—from sign language to making a soufflé—that you would like to have but know nothing about. Find out how to do this skill, either by reading a book or by talking to someone who can do it. Then teach it to your class. When you finish, write the steps to learning the skill and analyze how well you taught the class.

Extending Your Reading

Annie Sullivan is a well-known teacher because of her influence on Helen Keller, the blind-and-deaf girl whom Sullivan taught. Read one of the books below about Helen Keller and Annie Sullivan. Write five tips you learned about teaching from Annie Sullivan's work.

Helen Keller: Crusader for the Blind and Deaf, by Stewart Graff
The Helen Keller Story, by Catherine Owen Peare
Helen Keller: A Light for the Blind, by Kathleen Kudlinski
Helen Keller, by Richard Tames

20 BORN TO RUN

Bruce Springsteen is a big name in the rock-music world. But even with all his success, Springsteen does not rest on his laurels. He continues to experiment with musical styles. Some thought he had reached his peak with *Born to Run*. That album brought him fame and prosperity. In later albums, such as *Darkness on the Edge of Town* and *The River*, he continued to expand and refine his art. In 1986, Springsteen released a complete collection of his concert performances. Springsteen has been named artist of the year, best male vocalist, and best songwriter.

What is the secret of Springsteen's success? His music is a synthesis of the old and the new. Springsteen has been influenced by folk ballads and country laments. He takes stories about loners and losers and embellishes them with striking details and new rhythms.

Dressed in tight jeans and a leather jacket, Springsteen looks like a rebel. He leaps on tables and flails his arms and legs as he works his way through a song. His act is tough and raucous—and his audiences love it.

Springsteen's album *Nebraska* adds to his reputation as a maverick. At a time when punk rock and disco music were popular, he continued to go his own way. One critic called *Nebraska* "the bravest of Springsteen's records." It is a haunting folk album with instruments used sparingly in the background. The songs are part of the familiar Springsteen landscape—family problems, broken dreams, and losers on the run.

UNDERSTANDING THE STORY

>>>> *Circle the letter next to each correct statement.*

1. The statement that best expresses the main idea of this selection is:
   a. Bruce Springsteen continues to change and grow as a musician.
   b. Bruce Springsteen acts wildly on stage and has many fans.
   c. Bruce Springsteen music is a combination of folk rock and new wave.

2. The secret of Bruce Springsteen's success is
   a. his act is tough and wild.
   b. his songs are about losers and loners.
   c. he combines old musical styles with new rock energy.

117

MAKE AN ALPHABETICAL LIST

>>>> Here are the ten vocabulary words in this lesson. Write them in alphabetical order in the spaces below.

| laurels | laments | refine | flails | raucous |
| maverick | embellishes | haunting | prosperity | synthesis |

1. embellishes
2. flails
3. haunting
4. laments
5. laurels

6. maverick
7. prosperity
8. raucous
9. refine
10. synthesis

WHAT DO THE WORDS MEAN?

>>>> Following are some meanings, or definitions, for the ten vocabulary words in this lesson. Write the words next to their definitions.

1. haunting — remaining in one's memory; not easily forgotten

2. synthesis — a combination; a blending of different parts

3. raucous — loud and disorderly

4. maverick — a person who doesn't go along with the crowd; an individualist

5. prosperity — wealth; success

6. laments — sad or mournful tunes or verses; complaints

7. embellishes — makes more beautiful by adding something

8. laurels — honors a person has won for achievement

9. flails — swings wildly

10. refine — to improve; to make finer

COMPLETE THE SENTENCES

>>>> *Use the vocabulary words in this lesson to complete the following sentences. Use each word only once.*

prosperity	laments	haunting	embellishes	flails
refine	maverick	raucous	synthesis	laurels

1. Bruce Springsteen could rest on his _____laurels_____, but he enjoys writing new material.

2. The _____haunting_____ lyrics of *Nebraska* make this album hard to forget.

3. *Born to Run* brought Springsteen national fame and _____prosperity_____.

4. Springsteen's music is a _____synthesis_____ of folk music and modern rock.

5. He is famous for the way he _____flails_____ his arms and legs during a concert.

6. _____Laments_____ are usually sad but beautiful songs.

7. Only a _____maverick_____ such as Springsteen would make an album as unusual as *Nebraska*.

8. Springsteen will _____refine_____ a rough lyric until it is special.

9. He _____embellishes_____ standard forms by adding details and new rhythms.

10. The atmosphere at a Springsteen concert is _____raucous_____ and lively.

USE YOUR OWN WORDS

>>>> *Look at the picture. What words come into your mind? Write them on the lines below. To help you get started, here are two good words:*

1. _____singer_____
2. _____guitar_____
3. ___Answers will vary.___
4. _____
5. _____
6. _____
7. _____
8. _____
9. _____
10. _____

FIND THE ANALOGIES

>>>> In an **analogy,** similar relationships occur between words that are different. For example, *pig* is to *hog* as *car* is to *automobile*. The relationship is that the words have the same meaning. Here's another analogy: *noisy* is to *quiet* as *short* is to *tall*. In this relationship, the words have opposite meanings.

>>>> *See if you can complete the following analogies. Circle the correct word or words.*

1. **Prosperity** is to **poverty** as **strength** is to

   a. power   **b.** wealth   **c.** weakness   **d.** hunger

2. **Embellishes** is to **decorates** as **embezzles** is to

   a. steal   **b.** employ   **c.** embarrass   **d.** export

3. **Raucous** is to **loud** as **tranquil** is to

   a. regular   **b.** cheerful   **c.** disorderly   **d.** calm

4. **Synthesis** is to **combination** as **analysis** is to

   a. total   **b.** amount   **c.** separation   **d.** result

5. **Lament** is to **mourn** as **refine** is to

   a. charge   **b.** improve   **c.** file   **d.** define

COMPLETE THE STORY

>>>> Here are the ten vocabulary words for this lesson:

haunting	synthesis	maverick	laurels	prosperity
refine	flails	raucous	embellishes	laments

>>>> *There are six blank spaces in the story below. Four vocabulary words have already been used in the story. They are underlined. Use the other six words to fill in the blanks.*

Bruce Springsteen is considered a _____maverick_____ in the field of rock music. Though he underlines embellishes the work of others, his style is his own. In many ways, Springsteen's music is a complete _____synthesis_____ of the old and the new. He often takes a familiar idea and finds a way to refine it. The result is a beautiful, _____haunting_____ song that stays in the mind of the listener.

On stage, Springsteen flails his arms and legs. Crowds at his concerts sometimes react by becoming _____raucous_____. Yet, they can also be moved by the sad laments that he sings. These songs tell of people who do not know _____prosperity_____.

After so much success, Springsteen could rest on his _____laurels_____, but he finds his true pleasure in new songs.

Learn More About Rock Music

>>>> *On a separate sheet of paper or in your notebook or journal, complete one or more of the activities below.*

Building Language

Select a recording of a famous song from a muscian you like. Listen to the music and the lyrics. Then read the lyrics to the song (look in the CD or tape for a copy). Ask a friend to explain any phrases you do not understand. Write a summary of the story that the song is telling.

Learning Across the Curriculum

Musicians Woody Guthrie, Bob Dylan, and Hank Williams all influenced Bruce Springsteen's music. Listen to music by Springsteen and by the artists who influenced him. Explain how you think these artists influenced Springsteen's music.

Extending Your Reading

Read one of these books about famous rock musicians, or read another book about a musician whose music you enjoy. Then write what helped this person succeed and how his or her life influenced his or her music.

Elvis Presley: The King, by Katherine Krohn
Tina Turner, by D.L. Mabery
John Lennon, by Bruce Conord
Bruce Springsteen, by Ron Frankl

A

accessible *[ak SES uh bul]* within reach; easy to get at

accountable *[uh KOUN tuh bul]* responsible; answerable

achievers *[uh CHEEV urz]* people who accomplish something

adequate *[AD uh kwit]* just enough

adhered *[ad HEERD]* held closely; followed

adjacent *[ahd JAY sent]* near; connected

adjusted *[uh JUST uhd]* adapted; got used to

adolescents *[ah doh LES untz]* some teen-agers; young people between the ages of 12 and 17

adversaries *[AD vuh sair eez]* opponents; enemies

advocate *[AD vuh ket]* a person who defends or stands up for other people or a cause

aggressive *[uh GRES iv]* showing energy, ambition, and confidence

alcoholic *[al kuh HOL uhk]* a person who is dependent on alcohol

amiable *[AY mee uh buhl]* agreeable; friendly

ample *[AM puhl]* full or enough; plenty of something; generous

animated *[AN uh may tid]* moving as if alive

anthropologist *[an throh PAHL ah jist]* one who studies the customs and cultures of different peoples

ardent *[AHR dunt]* eager; filled with enthusiasm and feeling

assert *[uh SURT]* to declare; to state positively

asserted *[uh SURT id]* stated positively; said with confidence

assumes *[uh SOOMZ]* takes over; undertakes

astonished *[uh STON ishd]* amazed; greatly surprised

B

bereaved *[bee REEVD]* saddened by the death of a loved one; feeling a loss

C

carcass *[KAHR kus]* a dead body

casualties *[KAZH oo uhl teez]* people who have been harmed or killed

ceramics *[suh RAM iks]* the art of making pottery, usually from clay

citation *[seye TAY shun]* a formal statement that honors a person

combination *[kohm buh NAY shun]* mixture

comments *[KOM entz]* explanatory remarks; critical observations

comparable *[KOM pur uh bul]* similar; alike in some ways

complex *[kom PLEX]* having many parts; complicated

components *[kum POH nunts]* necessary parts; the parts that make up the whole

conclusions *[kon KLOO zhuns]* reasoned judgments; opinions based on facts

confirm *[kuhn FERM]* to approve; to remove doubt

conflicts *[KON flikts]* struggles; strong disagreements

conscientious *[kon she EN shus]* thoughtful; careful

contemporary *[kun TEM puh reh ree]* modern; of today

contempt *[kun TEMPT]* a feeling of dislike; having no respect or concern for another

contradictory *[kon truh DIK tur ee]* opposed; in disagreement with

contrasts *[KON trasts]* great differences

controversy *[KON truh vur see]* cause of disagreement or argument

corridor *[KOR uh dur]* a hallway that connects rooms

creed *[KREED]* a statement of belief

crusade *[kroo SAYD]* strong attempt to promote a cause or an idea

crypt *[KRIPT]* underground vault or chamber

cubism *[KYOO biz um]* a type of painting that uses only lines and simple shapes

D

dauntless *[DAWNT les]* brave

defective *[dee FEK tev]* faulty; lacking something essential

demolished *[dee MOL ishd]* destroyed; torn down

depicts *[dih PIKTS]* shows; represents

destiny *[DES tuh nee]* what happens to someone; fate

deterioration *[dih TIR ee uh RAY shun]* worsening of conditions or value

diligently *[DIL uh junt lee]* carefully, steadily, and earnestly

discharge *[DIHS charj]* to let go

dismiss *[dis MIS]* to disbelieve; to disregard

dispel *[dis PEL]* to clear away

disperse *[dih SPURS]* to scatter; to spread

E

elated *[eh LAYT uhd]* excited; joyful

elevates *[EL uh VAYTS]* raises to a higher level; improves

embellishes *[em BEL ish ez]* makes more beautiful by adding something

encounter *[en KOWN tur]* to meet face to face

enviable *[EN vee uh bul]* highly desirable; wanted by others

exalted *[eg ZAWLT id]* noble; grand and important

excel *[ek SEL]* to be better than others; to be superior

exquisite *[EKS kwiz it]* of exceptional quality, beauty, or detail

exterior *[eks TEER ee ur]* outside

F

fabric *[FA brik]* the structure; the quality (of something)

fantasy *[FAN tuh see]* make-believe; imagination

flails *[FLAYLS]* swings wildly

formidable *[FOR mih duh bul]* causing wonder or amazement because of size or greatness

fraught *[FRAWT]* accompanied by; full of

frenzy *[FREHN zee]* temporary madness; wild activity

G

garbed *[GAHRBD]* covered with clothing; dressed

geometric *[JEE uh MET rik]* made from or related to simple shapes

glamour *[GLAM ur]* exciting attractiveness; fascinating personal style

gripping *[GRIP ing]* strongly holding one's attention; fascinating

gruesome *[GROO som]* frightening and ugly

guardian *[GAHR dee un]* one who watches, protects, and takes care of

H

haunting *[HAWNT ing]* remaining in one's memory; not easily forgotten

heritage *[HEH ruh tij]* something passed from one generation to the next

hinder *[HIN dir]* to get in the way; to block

I

ignited *[ihg NEYET ehd]* set on fire

illusion *[ih LOO zhun]* a kind of trick that makes something look like it really exists

immersed *[ih MURSD]* absorbed; involved deeply

immune *[ih MYOON]* protected from something, usually a disease

imposing *[im POH zing]* impressive because of size or greatness; forcing one's opinions or actions upon another

impoverished *[im POV uh risht]* poor

impressive *[ihm PREHS ihv]* admirable; deserving credit

incentive *[ihn SENT ihv]* a reason for doing something

individuality *[in dih vij oo WAL uh tee]* qualities that make one person different from all others

infection *[in FEK shun]* the process of causing disease

ingenious *[in JEEN yus]* showing great originality and cleverness

inscriptions *[in SKRIP shunz]* words that are written or carved in stone to make them last

insight *[IN seyet]* judgment; clear understanding

intriguing *[in TREE ging]* very interesting; fascinating

inventive *[in VEN tiv]* creative; able to make new things

investment *[in VEST munt]* giving something, such as money, in hopes of getting back something valuable

L

labeled *[LAY buld]* described as

laborious *[luh BOR ee us]* involving or requiring very hard work

laments *[luh MENTS]* sad or mournful tunes or verses; complaints

laurels *[LAW rulz]* honors a person has won for achievement

leeway *[LEE way]* convenient room for freedom of action

literature *[LIT ur uh chur]* written works of art

lyrical *[LEER ih kul]* song-like; poetic

M

magnificent *[mag NIF ih sent]* grand; stately; splendid

magnitude *[MAG nuh tood]* size

maneuver *[muh NOO vur]* to direct or guide with skill

massive *[MAS iv]* large, solid, or heavy

maverick *[MAV rik]* a person who doesn't go along with the crowd; an individualist

menacing *[MEN uh sing]* dangerous; threatening

monorail *[MON uh rayl]* a kind of train that rides on only one track

morbid *[MOR bid]* very gloomy

mourned *[MORND]* grieved; felt sad over someone's death

multiple *[MUL tuh pul]* more than one; many

multitude *[MUL tuh tood]* a great number

N

navigable *[NAV uh guh bul]* wide and deep enough for travel by boat

neglected *[nih GLECT id]* not cared for; left unattended

O

obstinate *[OB stuh nit]* stubborn; set in one's ways

octagonal *[ok TA gun nol]* having eight sides

optical *[OP tuh kul]* having to do with vision or the eyes

ornate *[or NAYT]* having much detail; elaborate

overpower *[OH vur POW ur]* to defeat because of greater strength; to get the better of by force or power

P

paralyzed *[PEAR uh leyezd]* unable to move; made powerless

perfecting *[pur FEKT ing]* improving; bringing nearer to perfection

perfection *[per FEK shun]* freedom from errors; excellence

phenomena *[fih NOM uh nuh]* facts or events of scientific interest

phenomenal *[fih NOM uh nul]* something that strikes people as strange or uncommon; a visible appearance

plausible *[PLAW zuh bul]* believable; reasonable

politicians *[pawl ih TIHSH uhnz]* people who conduct the business of government

possibility *[paws uh BIHL uh tee]* something that may happen

precise *[pree SEYES]* exact

predator *[PRED uh tor]* an animal that kills other animals for food

prior *[PREYE uhr]* earlier; before

propels *[pruh PELZ]* pushes forward

prophecies *[PRO fih sees]* predictions; forecasts on the basis of religious inspiration
prosperity *[prah SPER uh tee]* wealth; success
provoke *[pruh VOHK]* to bring on an action
purification [pyoor uh fuh KAY shun] a cleansing; an act of removing anything that is improper, corrupt, or damaging
pyramid *[PEER uh mid]* an ancient structure, made of blocks, with a square bottom and four sides shaped like triangles that meet in a point at the top

R

raucous *[RAW kuhs]* loud and disorderly
ravenous *[RAV uh nus]* very hungry
reaction *[ree AK shuhn]* a response to something
reared *[REERD]* raised; brought up
recite *[ri SYT]* say from memory
recovery *[ree KUV uhr ee]* a return to normal
rectangular *[rek TANG yuh lur]* having four sides and four right angles
refine *[rih FYN]* to improve; to make finer
regal *[REE gul]* having to do with kings and queens; royal
registration *[rej ih STRAY shuhn]* enrollment; signing up
remorse *[ree MORS]* a disturbing feeling of guilt
renovation *[REN uh VAY shun]* the act of repairing something to look like new
replica *[REP luh kuh]* a copy
revived *[rih VYVD]* renewed; refreshed
ridicule *[RID uh kyool]* to laugh at or make fun of
ritual *[RICH oo wull]* a ceremony; an act done in a precise manner according to certain rules
robust *[roh BUST]* strong and healthy
ruthless *[ROOTH lis]* showing no mercy or pity

S

scorched *[SKORCHT]* burnt
scrutinize *[SKROO tun ize]* to look at closely; to examine
sculpture *[SKULP chur]* carved or molded artwork
sensitive *[SEN suh tuhv]* delicate; easily damaged
sequence *[SEE kwuhns]* items in a certain order
similarities *[SIM ih LAR ih teez]* likenesses; things that are almost the same
skyscraper *[SKY skray pur]* a very tall building
sponsored *[SPON sured]* supported; helped
stamina *[STAM uh nuh]* strength; ability to bear fatigue or pain
strategies *[STRAD uh jeez]* careful or clever plans to reach a goal
stricken *[STRIK un]* hit or hurt, usually by a disease or misfortune
subtle *[SUH tul]* skillful; artful; delicately crafted
successful *[suk SES ful]* having achieved something attempted

suite *[SWEET]* a series of musical movements that vary in number and character
sundry *[SUN dree]* various; miscellaneous
superb *[suh PERB]* excellent
swerves *[SWERVZ]* moves off a straight course; turns aside
synthesis *[SIN thu sis]* a combination; a blending of different parts

T

Talmud *[TAL mood]* the writings of Jewish law and history
tarnished *[TAHR nihshd]* made dirty; stained
technique *[tek NEEK]* a method of or skill in doing something
tenants *[TEN unts]* renters; people who occupy property owned by another
tenement *[TEN uh munt]* an apartment building
titanic *[ty TAN ik]* very big and powerful
torment *[TOR ment]* suffering; great pain
trait *[TRAYT]* a distinguishing quality; a characteristic
tuition *[too ISH un]* money paid to go to a school

U

undeniable *[un dih NY uh bul]* plainly true; not questionable
universal *[yoo nuh VUR sul]* worldwide; belonging to or having to do with all people
unteachable *[un TEECH uh bul]* not able to be taught
uttered *[UT uhrd]* pronounced; spoken

V

vaccine *[vak SEEN]* a medical preparation that prevents disease
vandalizing *[VAN dul eyez ing]* intentionally damaging or destroying property
vanquished *[VANG kwisht]* defeated
varied *[VAIR eed]* different; of many types
verdict *[VER dekt]* a judgment or an opinion
verify *[VER uh fy]* to agree or prove that something is true
virus *[VEYE rus]* something within body cells that causes disease
vitality *[vy TAL uh tee]* energy; liveliness

W

wend *[WEND]* to travel; to move along a route
wrongfully *[RONG ful lee]* unjustly; unfairly

Z

zeal *[ZEEL]* eagerness; passion